Divinity in a Grain of Bread

Divinity
in a
Grain of Bread

David Martin

Foreword by the
Archbishop of Canterbury

Lutterworth Press
Cambridge

Lutterworth Press
P. O. Box 60
Cambridge CB1 2NT

British Library Cataloguing in Publication Data
Martin, David, 1929-
    Divinity in a Grain of Bread.
    1. Christian life. Devotional works
    I. Title
    242

    ISBN 0-7188-2787-2

Copyright © David Martin 1989
First published 1989 by Lutterworth Press

Printed in Great Britain by
The Guernsey Press Co. Ltd, Guernsey, Channel Islands

Dedication

For Thomas Cranmer, Archbishop
born 1489 martyred 1556

Contents

Foreword

The accepted wisdom is that we do not live in an age of preaching. Collections of sermons, big sellers in the reign of Victoria, are rarely published nowadays. Yet someone recently estimated that at least 40,000 sermons are preached every Sunday in the churches of England. The sermon remains the main source of Christian instruction for the vast majority of the Church's members. Its value in forming Christian minds and shaping Christian discipleship should never be underestimated.

This collection of David Martin's addresses illustrates the sermon's enduring value. Here we find orthodox Christian doctrine imaginatively expounded, and illuminated from the worlds of art, literature and history. As we would expect from such a distinguished sociologist, there is a clear understanding of the Christian's place in society and the power of community to shape our lives and attitudes. David Martin is also known for his love of the Book of Common Prayer. That is reflected in his own use of language which, whilst contemporary, is refreshing in form and style.

Many of these sermons were delivered in the context of the Eucharist. We have grown to appreciate the links between Word and Sacrament. The Eucharist is proclamation as well as celebration. The preached word may impart a grace which is properly called sacramental. These addresses consistently point away from the preacher and draw us out of ourselves towards the God whom to serve is perfect freedom.

The Most Reverend Robert Runcie
Archbishop of Canterbury

Preface

This small 'body of divinity' consists of meditations, mainly on the Eucharist and on fundamental Christian beliefs, delivered at Guildford Cathedral between 1984 and 1986 and during 1988 and 1989. During that time I was an honorary assistant at the Cathedral, thanks to the kindness of the Dean, Anthony Bridge, and his colleagues. My life alternated between the London School of Economics during the week and the Cathedral on Sundays.

These meditations grew out of the traditional Anglican liturgy embodied in the Book of Common Prayer. They refer back to the poetry and doctrine of the Prayer Book and deploy the language of the Authorized (King James) version of the English Bible. But they also attempt to translate the traditional language and the central doctrines, in particular by exploiting the meanings and roots of words. Liturgies the world over play with words and are built on profound puns. Great preachers, like Lancelot Andrewes, have done the same. I have tried to follow in that tradition.

This is not a scholarly book, though it is serious and at times quite concentrated. As a result I have omitted any scholarly apparatus, including the careful correction and acknowledgement of all quotations. Sermons, like the Bible itself, are mosaics of quotation, and annotation is not only pretentious but disrupts the flow. So I have not indicated every occasion when I have glancingly utilized a fragment from T.S. Eliot or Gerard Manley Hopkins or drawn - to give an example which bothers me more - on Wilfrid Mellers for my discussion of the theology and meaning of music. I have not even attempted to remove all traces of the particular 'emergent occasions' on which these pieces were delivered, since they were, after all, part of an ecclesiastical cycle or church year which runs through a time sequence.

Almost all the meditations were given in Guildford Cathedral and under certain constraints: ten minutes - occasionally five

- for an address in the course of the Eucharist, fifteen minutes for an address in Mattins or Evensong. As may be noticed, the Cathedral combined the traditional lectionary and ecclesiastical year with recent innovations in a slightly unusual way. The two flanking meditations, namely Prologue and Epilogue, suffered no time constraints and were given respectively in Canterbury, at the invitation of the Dean of Canterbury, the Very Reverend Victor de Waal, and in Perkins Chapel, Southern Methodist University, Dallas, Texas.

I would like to take the opportunity to express my thanks to the Very Reverend Alex Wedderspoon for his kindness and encouragement as Dean of Guildford from 1987 onwards. My thanks are due also to Dr Andrew Walker of the C. S. Lewis Centre for his help and assistance.

David Martin

Prologue:
Worship, an Invitation*

Worship is a form of engagement and an invitation. Yet it rarely speaks to you directly. Worship has implicit, inviting patterns, not crude and obvious shapes. The shape of the liturgy and the meanings of it stay partly covered; almost covert.

So worship is a slightly indirect invitation to commence a certain kind of engagement. The invitation is a call and a process of approach. Take first the calling, because it is often the most miraculous part of worship. Indeed, it is perfectly possible for the whole act of worship to be completed in a momentary response to that call. Sometimes I stand in my garden or in the city street and hear a solitary bell. Perhaps the ringer thinks that no real approach is made from his side or from mine. Not at all. A complete dialogue has occurred between an inner vibration and that bell. Worship can have a resonance of one second. I become a moment of receptivity and immobility. When men are summoned by bells, the mind makes obeisance in a moment of collective turning.

Collective turning. Let me look first at the *common* approach which initiates worship. When I, as individual, receive the summons, it is important that I am summoned to a *common* prayer. The act I contemplate involves joining with others across time and space. My forebears said this prayer; my contemporaries utter this prayer too. It is a double chain sideways and backwards. The identical prayers mediate my identity and my identification, allowing me to attest present and past together.

———————

*The author would like to thank *Theology* for permission to reprint the Prologue.

That is not only true of what passes the lips, but it frames the act of walking towards the house of prayer. When I begin that walk, I share a common orientation. I look east. My soul and body are turned eastward just as the sacred building itself is turned eastward.

In that last sentence, I used the passive: are turned, is turned. That is very important and it reflects a difficult but essential piece of theology: the idea of prevenient grace. Grace goes before you and you are turned. The moment of turning is peculiar because the mind is often very unwilling and resistant. At the moment we walk towards the sacred enclosure and equally while we are there we are turned and drawn. Passivity is one of the essentials of liturgical action. The *opus Dei*, the work of God is in a peculiar voice: the active-passive. It invites and indicates more than it exhorts.

All I have said so far concerns invitations, biddings, approaches, orientations, turnings. So we are still at the turning point. Another word for turning point is conversion. I don't mean a dramatic reversal of a life-way, but a quiet visitation. The visit which we propose to make to the temple is actually a visitation made to us. What we take to be a step forward made by us is a step already taken. That is why Christian mythology is so full of visitations and messengers. *Angelus ad virginem inquit 'Ave'*. The angel greets the virgin with 'Hail'. The virgin answers: 'Be it unto me according to thy word.' The miracle of visitation and response is already accomplished before we stir. As Elijah sleeps the angel has already prepared his food. As Israel sleeps the manna has already fallen on the ground. As Peter sleeps the prison door has been opened.

This going to the temple, drawn by prevenient grace, has something almost joyfully Jewish and Old Testament about it. 'For my brethren and my companion's sake I will go to the house of the Lord.' The moment of approach is as much worship as anything we do when we arrive. There is a tailing away of ordinary concerns, and a dropping of mundane chat or everyday tittle-tattle. Things alter. That is because this building contains and embodies a shift of perspective, an extended horizon, an altered view. It belongs to that which is 'other': a house but not any house. Though everything *can* be made holy, this building focuses and channels our sense of 'hallowing'. The place we stand on is designated holy ground and we are 'here to kneel where prayer has been valid'.

Even when you enter an ordinary house there is a shift of comportment. You alter your gait, pause, give and receive greetings, wait maybe to be conducted into the inner sanctum. This is the great defect of Protestantism that the concern with an inner disposition is at the expense of outward acts. Merely to touch the holy water is a mark of respect which acknowledges identity and belonging.

It is precisely that outward gesture which will inform the inward disposition. To begin with the quest for sincerity is to place a weight on subjectivity under which it may collapse. The external act frames and supports the inner sense. This is how men achieve and receive an awareness of liminality, or the crossing of thresholds. They are carried across by gestures or a special stance. The unbeliever is inducted into this as well as the believer, unless he makes a positive decision to exclude himself. The objective external character of the physical threshold inducts him into a distinctive world where he may be touched by momentary recollection or by a thankfulness that other things are here remembered and celebrated. He does not have to ask at that moment 'And is it true? and is it true?' because it is enough to recognize a difference which embodies a vision. To eliminate that difference or to reduce the distinctive threshold is not (as some suppose) to universalize a vision, but to eliminate it.

What happens inside a church if you should consent to worship with the faithful can only be hinted at, because the symbolic concentration is so dense. In any case the various inner worlds of people move at different speeds, and they obey different patterns. The pattern followed by priest is not necessarily all that closely aligned with the patterns which form in the worlds of the worshippers. For the worshipper the range of symbolic action may reduce itself to 'Lord, I am not worthy, but speak the word only'.

Or it may be the simple and solitary act of obeisance at the moment of consecration. All that is needed for a valid act of prayer is recognition of a presence, the re-cognition of Presence, inspiring the acknowledgement of unworthiness or the moment of obeisance.

A service can begin dramatically with an announcement 'The Lord is here' or with a greeting 'The Lord be with you' or an acclamation 'Alleluia'. It may commence more indirectly with a statement of intent or invitation. One of the most beautiful of all statements of intent is 'I will go in unto the altar of God, unto God who giveth joy to my youth'. *Introibo ad altare Dei.* You have sentences of indirect invitations in morning and evening prayer and they are like small, beautifully shaped pointers, gentle indications, terse reminders and warnings. At the beginning of morning prayer we hear 'Enter not into judgement with thy servant, O Lord, for in thy sight shall no man be justified'.

These indirections or statements of intent are appropriated sideways. You share in a meditative moment initiated by the priest, but he is not talking *to* you. He is himself acknowledging a signal even as he makes it. You are conjoined with him, and make an act of alignment with the direction he indicates. The priest has not begun a simple dialogue with you, one to one, but has initiated a pattern in which he sometimes turns to you asking for an act of alignment, and then turns away so that you with him, face toward that which judges and transcends. All the different ways in which a priest celebrates, whether away from or facing or standing sideways to the congregation, embody this turning away from and turning towards. At the present time, there is an accent on turning towards as a basis for dialogue, but no worship which is truly worship can avoid indicators which turn upwards or away.

But what of the indicators which turn inwards? Here we enter on an arena of disagreement, because worship can embody different polarities in different ways. 'Away from' and 'towards' represent one polarity. The inward and the outward represent another polarity which is closely linked with the polarity between active and passive. Then there is the question of whether signs and

4

symbolic acts should be 'natural' or not. The present shifts have been towards the outward-going, the active, the facing towards, and the natural. Outwardness, face to face activity and naturalness all bring into play profound theological issues, even political ones which I cannot discuss here. There are those who argue that if the people of God must realize their faith politically then outward and active gestures should predominate over inward and passive ones.

Yet there exists an inward journey to the invisible and eternal as well as an outward movement towards temporal and mundane activity. Recollection and meditation are aspects of prayer in which the mind is allowed to settle and achieve emptiness, or clarity or plenitude. Here again, what primarily matters is not what you believe, but willingness to let be. Prayer in this mode means to let be and to let alone. It may happen at any moment, whatever else is occurring in the objective pattern of the rite. The mind may fill or empty, or be 'soft sift in an hour glass'. The self discovers itself, uncovers and recovers. And this inward condition is made possible by the outward disposition of the body. The closing of eyes is that infolding and flowering of the spirit. The kneeling man because he kneels makes transfiguration possible. He cannot command it, and it is dangerous directly to seek it. Everything is in the waiting. Prayer is a waiting on God. This, once again, is passive: 'I waited for the Lord: he inclined unto me.'

This inner quiet, defended from intrusion and noisy camaraderie, is central to worship. Of course, the mind also rejoins the communal celebration and aligns itself with a shared text. This shared text is what is meant by common prayer and ideally it is something you know by heart and which you have repeated hundreds of times. It should have rhythm, urgency, spiritual energy, and a sense of cumulative power, so that the mind may rest in it and also be carried forward. The self scans and monitors the sacred text, absorbing and appropriating a poetry of faith. So far as may be, this is an impersonal process, undisturbed by intrusive emphasis on this aspect or on that. The impersonal recitation of the immemorial text allows the mind to spring free and take whatever is required. At the same time, the common iteration and reiteration accepts solidarity with past and present. The self both discovers itself an inner identity and also embraces solidarity with others.

But, of course, these recoveries of self and alignments with others are indirect because they are mediated. The media of worship provide a circuit within which different kinds of contact are possible. Moreover, the circuit is 'looped' through an objective 'other'. You do not just talk to yourself or talk to others, but you place yourself so that which is 'not self' can be manifest and make you more complete. You and others accept the mediation of the transcendent through the text and the pattern of action.

The inner quiet depends on the indirect contact through this double mediation provided by a rite which stands objectively 'out there' and a Being who stands 'out there'. The Communion exists to provide the objective, automatic, totally reliable and expected frame which allows free passage for the soul. The individual does *not* so much express the soul's sincere desire as assent to an occurrence which may inform his being and conform it to a certain image and likeness. Likewise, the Being 'out there' is not some subjective spasm or dredged up sincerity but *He who is.* You would not seek him if you had not already found him. Even the seeking is not always necessary. All that is required is an interior assent to a possibility and a potentiality. There is an otherness which provides the frame and the means and the medium, by which the self may express itself in not-self. In the words of Gerard Manley Hopkins it rises and sinks to what 'bodes and abides'. The key words are the prepositions *in, through* and *by.* Every now and again the rite is held together and the self taken into it by these powerful linkages: *in* whom, *by* whom, and *through* whom in the unity of the Holy Ghost, be all honour and glory.

To allow the possibility and potentiality of this linking and this objective Presence is also to engage in the profound abasement which precedes exaltation. Again, this abasement has nothing to do with feelings, subjective grovelling or guiltiness. The confession is not there for us to express disquiet. It is there for an acknowledgement of the common human condition. 'We have erred and strayed from thy ways. We have followed too much the devices and desires of our own hearts. We have offended against thy holy laws.' All this is an acknowledgement and recognition of the distance which separates us from all that is holy, and yet it is made in full assurance. The lowering precedes being raised. These profound prayers of separation, distance and alienation are a preparation which already anticipates union and acceptance. We know all the time that our life is a constant falling away and a being sustained, and taken back. Profound abasement and acceptance are almost simultaneous. Sometimes you may *feel* both, but ordinarily you acknowledge both without trying to reproduce appropriate subjective responses. How you feel doesn't matter.

Abasement and exaltation. Let me repeat St Paul's words: 'I know how to be exalted and I know how to be abased.' Exaltation means what it says: the high point and summit of the act of worship. *Altus* is that which is high. The words which belong together in this context are exaltation, elation and elevation. The climax is a raising aloft and presenting in a moment of sacrifice and oblation which becomes a moment of union. The whole of faith is encapsulated in acts of self-emptying which are then taken up and transfigured. It is death and resurrection. The priest, acting as representative, is identified with a crucified God and pleads that sacrifice, partaking in death, resurrection and exaltation. The symbolic gestures here are so concentrated and dense, and so interlinked and folded one in to the other that you cannot really describe a settled sequence. The self-giving of the human is joined to the self-giving of the divine. This wipes out the distance between men and God, allowing God to be taken into man, received under signs of bread and wine, and manhood to be taken into God. At the moment of breakage, symbolized by fracture, there is healing and wholeness. Our brokenness breaks God, and his brokenness makes us whole.

Here we need three more related words: whole, hale and holy. The recovery of wholeness through breakage and brokenness unveils the Presence of God. We, with Christ, the representative Man, enter into the heavenly places. 'Seeing we have a great high

priest who has passed into the heavens, Jesus the Son of God . . .'
Christ as Representative Man enters the holy of holies.

This heavenly entry has two moments: silence and fullness. If
you listen to the profound commentaries by the great musicians on
this point in the pattern of worship, you hear the shift. First there
is the collapse of all articulate speech in wonder. Mortal mind
stands transfixed, immobilized, overawed, breath itself almost
suspended. The spirit still lies under the shadow of the presence.
There begins a slow enveloping movement, a pressure which
steals forward with a sense of ecstatic containment. Then containment breaks out in tongues of fire, which fill the house. The
receptive silence is now engulfed in sound: heaven and earth are
full. Everything in heaven and earth is pointed towards its consummation.

The consummation itself is the universal banquet in the
Kingdom of God. Of course, from beginning to end the whole of
eucharistic worship can be viewed as a simple meal. The essence
is a giving thanks, establishing a vertical dimension, and a
distribution, establishing a horizontal dimension. Hence the constant movement of priestly hands, making and establishing the
horizontal and vertical arms of the Cross. At one moment the
elements are raised to God, at another given to men. It is triangular
solidarity between the Godhead and humankind.

But that solidarity is not merely pointed upwards and sideways. It looks forward and back, which makes it totally inclusive,
covering every dimension in time and space. The backward look
is an anamnesis, or remembering: do this in memory of me.
Remote time is recalled and recovered in the present.

The forward look is an anticipation. In the past a body was
broken that men might be whole. Still that wholeness is not
realized, because men remain broken and separated. They break
inwardly and they break fellowship, one with another. But in the
feast of consummation, men are healed inwardly and their fellowship is universally established. It is not a matter of converting
everyone to a religion, and persuading them to join a church, but
of envisaging and presaging a Kingdom. The final visions of the

supper of the lamb have to do with human unity, not some institutional triumph. The Church remains a channel or focus for the interim, simply carrying that vision forward in explicit form. The elements in the vision are reciprocity, sharing, joy, celebration, abundance, fullness.

The elements of bread and wine are signs of the body, first the body of Christ broken for men and by men, and second the body of men united in Him through redeeming love. They represent and re-present His body and life entering into their body and life. His body is food and manna to be received outwardly and fed upon inwardly. This divine life, poured out, is absorbed by humanity, and men are taken into God. God in man by entering into man takes manhood into deity. The sacrament itself repeats the movement of the incarnation. Incarnation means 'in the body', so the spirit of love is taken into the body and informs it throughout. Where it was impure it now becomes pure. In that act the worshipper is washed and covered, not because of what he is but by his readiness to receive. He is now in Luther's words: *simul iustus et peccator* - sinner yet justified. He pleads the gift as his sole justification, and if he offers anything else except readiness to receive a gift, he ceases to be justified. The situation is identical with human love: everything turns purely and solely on the gift and the reception: 'sufficient, sovereign, saving grace'.

How is the plea made? The priest acting as representative of the whole corporate body of those who receive the body of the Lord offers up the gift which is God to God as a sacrifice. That is, the sacrifice which a man raises up is the divine gift of life through death. Love lives eternally and rises above death because it is open to everything which may happen to it, being totally vulnerable. The priest who holds up the cup of blood places between himself and justice or wrath the wounds of love. He pleads the passion, and therefore achieves atonement. The sacrifice is also and simultaneously himself. By being joined to God through Christ in atonement, he is already part of love's sacrifice. 'We here present unto Thee our souls and bodies . . .'

Of course, it is impossible to tell how much of this texture of

9

meaning is grasped: the body of Christ under and in symbolic form; and the restoration from death in sin to life in God. That life is eternal. Those who kneel receptively and take the holy sacrament hear words which tell them to take it for their comfort and at the same time to enter into eternal life. So in a sense this simple meal, once absorbed, is a medicine of immortality. Or, to put it in more Christian terms, the sacrament is a foretaste of resurrection. There are two signs here. One is that of a man grafted into God, who finds life and immortality in the divine being. This suggests the image of the True Vine of which all members are the branches. The other image is of the seed of corn which sinks into the body, dies and then is raised. One image suggests a continuity whereby men are held in the being of God. The other image suggests a miraculous change in which this body will be raised in glory. Both images beggar the imagination. So it is useless to try and give them some comprehensible form and plausible location. We already have the bare signs, in the Vine and the Seed, the Wine and the Bread of Heaven. The imagination feeds on them and on them alone, since 'eye hath not seen nor ear hath not heard.'

Once the access, entry and reception are over, there are two directions in which a man may travel. Either he may contemplate the fact of coming: 'Blessed is he that cometh . . .' Or he may break out into the song of the angels: 'Glory to God in the Highest.' Both are entirely satisfactory conclusions. To contemplate the gift through absorption in prayer is natural. To pray as well for the gracious receipt of the whole act of prayer and thanksgiving is appropriate: 'O Lamb of God that taketh away the sins of the world, Receive our prayer.' To pray for inner and outer peace is a natural conclusion: 'O Lamb of God that taketh away the sins of the world, Grant us thy peace.'

But better still to break into the angelic hymn. God has visited and redeemed His people and He has fed them with the food of angels. This visitation transforms the whole creation, and sets it in peaceable order. The *Gloria* turns first to heaven and then to peace on earth: *Gloria in excelsis Deo: et in terra pax.* 'We praise thee. We bless thee, we glorify thee, we give thanks to thee for thy great glory, Lord God, Heavenly King, God the Father Almighty.' The whole earth is included in this transformation, transfiguration and transubstantiation.

All *Gloria in excelsis* cry!
Erd, air, fire, water, man and beast
He that is crowned above the sky
Pro nobis puer natus est

In other words, the complete embodiment is here and the whole creation awaits it in suffering and with expectation.

Go: the conclusion of the Eucharist is a sending out. *Ite, missa est:* the Latin means sent, and indicates 'mission'. This is the underlying alternation of worship between passivity and activity. Most of what happens in worship has to do with receptivity. The actions in which we engage indicate our willingness to receive and be open to pure gift. But the conclusion of that openness and reception is a command. It is part of discipline and discipleship to make real the symbolic banquet and to distribute the universal feast.

The alternation between reception and activity is also an alternation between dependence and autonomy. To be truly autonomous is to refuse to erect a protective screen between self and world. Much religious experience retires behind this screen. The screen is, of course, necessary, because it suggests the idea of protection. For example, the prayer to be defended this night from all assaults of our enemies invokes the sense of being cared for and guarded. It is very human and proper to pray for guardianship. But it is also childlike. An autonomous person looks after himself and faces experience directly. He does not cripple himself morally by constant leaning. We have to face anything there may be, for good or ill, without protection. It is just not true that God will look after us. He is not a convenient shield against reality. We must in one sense be fully human by taking it all alone, and deciding according to our personal judgement. Christianity is not a device for off-loading responsibility.

But, at the same time, we must achieve total trust and dependence. To depend on somebody is to risk your whole life on and for them. There is nothing so demanding and difficult as absolute trust, because we would fall to pieces if we were wrong.

Faith, however, is precisely this. It has nothing to do with the abnegation of reason or the fear of adulthood. It has to do with the most dangerous activity in which we may engage, which is trusting and being utterly prepared to receive. The autonomous man is prepared to receive even *this*. God Himself is the gift, the sense of miracle presented and made available to those who are not afraid to see or to be.

PART I
THE CHRISTIAN YEAR:
ADVENT TO TRINITY

Advent: 1.
The Quickening

'Prepare and make ready.'
Collect for Advent 3 (Book of Common Prayer)

Advent is traditionally understood as a time of quickened preparation and readiness 'for a birth and a death', for a beginning and an end. We are asked to expect God to come to us in weakness and in power, in fullness of grace and in judgement. We are to look for the child; we may also expect the King. The countenance of 'the Christ who is to be' takes on a double aspect. In the womb of Mary there is the helpless child. In the womb of time there is 'One like to the Son of Man, girt about the paps with a golden girdle, whose hairs are white as wool and whose eyes are as a flame of fire'. On the one hand our earthly existence is affirmed and our human flesh fulfilled with divinity; on the other hand all the pretences, corruptions and comfortable defences are burnt away and consumed.

This double aspect of Advent is not just a contrast in theology which is built into the liturgical year. Like all liturgy and all serious theology, it reflects and meets the poles of our experience. The child and the judge correspond to the unearnt gift and the unavoidable sifting. We know the gift of God and are tried in the furnace. We know what it is to have come on a journey which brought us into the presence of an inexplicable radiance, encountered as pure gift. And we also know what it is to find our worlds blasted, and our very being probed and sifted.

Nor is this response to gift and sense of sifting solely confined to climaxes. It is continuous. Each day may bring gift or test or both. Every moment may contain grace and terrifying collapse and fragmentation.

The gift and the dissolution are present in the individual life and in the life of whole nations. Sir Michael Tippett was speaking on television recently about his music. He called himself a divine go-between, and he described his art as moving between his experience of the poles of radiance and terrifying dissolution. Had you visited the exhibition of German twentieth-century painting at the Royal Academy, you would have seen a pictorial record of a whole society being drawn towards terror and dissolution. Whirls of paint are sucked in uncontrollable spirals towards the vortex. A picture of the prodigal son shows him beyond any hope of return. Hideous and threatening images point towards apocalypse.

And what happened in that society is not some peculiar sifting or some special judgement located elsewhere. Everywhere and at all times the radiance is possible and the dissolution lies in wait. For Germany (or Britain for that matter) read Nineveh and Tyre. The images of hope and sifting in the Bible are continuous with our contemporary experience. We respond to pictures of dissolution contained in the Bible as if they belonged to a special sacred world and as if apocalypse were always then and never now. You would hardly think, at least in our cosy family celebrations of Christmas, that we ourselves were poised individually between the gift and the test, or that as a civilization we were poised between radiance and atomic radiation.

Advent - what is *coming*, is the theme of the whole Bible, and in sacred scripture we are offered every image of terror and hope. The Bible, to our great and continual discomfort, is full of reminders of the rod of iron and the sickle that is soon to be thrust in. The Bible is marked by the hammer and by the sickle. 'The Lord will suddenly come to His temple. But who may abide the day of His coming? And who will stand when He appeareth? For He is like a refiner's fire and like a hammer that breaketh the rock.' If our Christmas cards told the whole truth, the berries would also clearly be images of blood. If the Advent candles are allowed to offer all their meaning, they would speak of the light but also of the fire. Advent is the season of the candle and the berry, *and* of the premonitory signs of blood and fire.

Advent is the moment in the human story and in our experience when the clock is just about to strike twelve. And as the clock moves towards midnight, all the images of terror and grace begin

16

to emerge from the womb of time. The sea and the waves roar. The fig tree puts forth its shoots. The watchman is on the tower of the city. The trumpets begin to blow at the round earth's imagined corners. The voice cries at midnight. And those images are transformed into the picture of the bridegroom seeking his bride. 'Arise my love, my fair one, and come away.' We see Christ the rose of Sharon and Christ the apple tree. The eagle rises with healing in his wings. The ancient of days becomes but two hours old; and he who made the fire now fears the cold.

In Advent we have to look for a child who brings joy and tears, water and blood and fire. Robert Southwell, the Catholic martyr, had a poetic vision of the Christ child coming at midwinter which he called the Burning Babe. It is a strange poem, but it has all the elements of Advent: the fire, the tearful flood, the furnace, and the blood.

The Burning Babe

As I in hoary winter's night stood shivering in the snow,
Surprised I was with sudden heat which made my heart to
  glow;
And lifting up a fearful eye to view what fire was near,
A pretty Babe all burning bright did in the air appear;
Who, scorched with excessive heat, such floods of tears did
  shed,
As though his floods should quench his flames which with his
  tears were fed.
'Alas!' quoth he, 'but newly born in fiery heats I fry,
Yet none approach to warm their hearts or feel my fire but I.
My faultless breast the furnace is, the fuel wounding thorns;
Love is the fire, and sighs the smoke, the ashes shame and
  scorns;
The fuel justice layeth on, and mercy blows the coals;
The metal in this furnace wrought are men's defiled souls:
For which, as now on fire I am to work them to their good,
So will I melt into a bath to wash them in my blood.'
With this he vanished out of sight and swiftly shrunk away,
And straight I called unto mind that it was Christmas day.

Advent: 2.
Coming-to-be

'All the prophets . . . have likewise foretold of these days.'
Acts 3:24

The theme is prophecy, and in particular how Christ was the fulfilling of prophecy. But what is prophecy and how is it fulfilled in Christ?

There are, of course, many kinds of prophecy. One is of a kind found in the Old Testament and which rather resembled a charismatic gathering today. The prophets gathered together in bands and were infused with shared ecstasy. They were taken out of themselves and into the spirit. Another kind of prophecy, found pre-eminently in the Old Testament, castigates the generation of the time for seeking after false gods, for indulging in luxury and sensuality, and for showing contempt for the poor, the widowed, and the fatherless. Yet another kind of prophecy is one where the prophet has foresight and descries what is to be. This perhaps is the conventional idea of a prophet. Certainly it is the kind spoken of in the Book of Deuteronomy, chapter 18. The writer of Deuteronomy has no doubt that you can tell a true prophet from a false one by whether or not his word comes to pass. If he foretells correctly he is God's spokesman; if not you may disregard him as uninspired. 'If the thing follow not, nor come to pass . . . the prophet hath spoken it presumptuously; thou shalt not be afraid of him.'

I want to think about *this* kind of prophet: the teller of things which will come to be. You might say of this particular prophetic style that it requires good anticipation, and quick footwork about the future. But there are obviously problems about this. It is so easy to have the wrong idea about the prophet who speaks of the future and anticipates what is to come. A prophet foretells, certainly, but not every foreteller is a prophet. We mustn't confuse prophecy with every kind of fortune-telling.

Were the Romans, who foresaw the outcome of a battle in the entrails of a fowl, prophets? Is the astrologer, who knows the benign or malign conjunctions of the stars, prophetic? If so, the London 'Evening Standard' regularly prints quite a lot of prophecy. Old Moore's Almanack could count as one of the prophetic books. A visit to Madame Sosostris, clairvoyante, could do the same for you as a reading of the prophet Isaiah. After all, they all speak of what is to be. Yet when you listen to what the crystal-gazer says and what Isaiah says it is something completely different. 'The Standard' writes: 'After a long period of disappointments over payments you should be able to extract binding promises now.' Perhaps 'Old Moore' will tell you who is to be assassinated in 1989. Useful information that - but not prophecy. Isaiah says:

> And the sucking child shall play on the hole of the asp, and the
> weaned child shall put his hand in the cockatrice' den.
> They shall not hurt nor destroy in all my holy mountain,
> For the earth shall be full of the knowledge of the Lord as the
> waters cover the sea.

What Old Moore offers is a prediction based on the notion of fatality: *che sará sará*. What Isaiah offers is a transforming vision of a world renewed. Lots of people try to read the biblical prophets as if they were Hebrew versions of Old Moore. American radio and television are deluged with dotty people who read the Bible like an Almanack of predictions.

The fatalism which underlies Old Moore is in fact the reverse of true prophecy, and dangerous if taken seriously. If we knew fate in advance we might cease to strive to bring about the transforming vision. Prophecy is vision, not fatalism or fatality. It invites us to follow after the vision: 'Arise, shine, for thy light is come.' 'Get thee up into the high mountain.' The future comes towards us with half-formed shapes which fade away fainter and fainter to an open horizon of hope.

The prophet takes us up into the high mountain to look toward that open horizon, and sees there the towers of the Eternal King. He is one who looks forward to things; he is full of anticipation; he is in travail with a possible future; he is expectant; he entertains hope. He has, as it were, a centre of gravity or a lodestone, about how things are disposed. On the one hand he has good anticipation, on the other he anticipates the good; he desires to see and he sees with desire. His desire helps bring the future into being.

No prophets actually foresaw the Christ Child. Out of the dim half-formed shapes coming towards them, they simply envisioned different towers of light. They looked forward to a new law written on the heart, to all nations flowing to the house of prayer, to a valley of dry bones come alive, to a mountain where no one is hurt or destroyed, to a voice in the wilderness, to a servant suffering for God's purposes, to a King in Zion, to the Lord of Hosts entering the uplifted gates of Jerusalem. All these were distant markers on a horizon of hope.

Here, too, was a pattern on which others, in later generations, were able to draw. Hundreds of years later, Christ was able to understand His mission and make Himself understood in terms of these markers. At the very beginning of His ministry He could open the book of prophecy, read it, and say to His hearers, 'Today, is this scripture fulfilled in your ears.' He could say, 'Abraham rejoiced to see my day.' He entered the world of their expectation and brought together the whole pattern the prophets had built up.

And the disciples were able to do the same, precisely because they saw the things He did as fulfilling 'all that the prophets had spoken'. Constantly they said: 'All the prophets . . . have foretold these days . . . . All this was done that it might be fulfilled.' Of course, it was also surprising and not quite what had been expected, yet, nevertheless, God was with His people, Emmanuel.

All the journeys of expectation ended unexpectedly and more marvellously *here* - in the birth of a child, and in the death of God's suffering servant. It was not only prophecy but God Himself 'coming-to-be'. So, as they retold the story, they in turn wove all the prophecies into it. Time and again the ancient prophecies were used to frame their own fulfilment in the Christian scriptures. The writer of the New Testament wrote 'as it was written'.

And we, in turn, now in the weeks before Christmas frame our own anticipations in terms of those prophecies, and refer back to those visionary markers. We look forward with Abraham, in whose seed the nations are to be blessed; with Moses on Sinai and Mt Pisgah; with Jesse out of whose stem comes the Christ; with Isaiah who saw the ransomed of the land returning with everlasting joy on their heads; with Zechariah who saw the King meekly coming to His own. We let the prophecies speak our own looking forward to Christmas, and we use their voice for our own longing to know and to see what is even now coming to be.

Christmas.
The Human Gift

'... Emmanuel ... God with us.'
St. Matthew 1:23

When I was first ordained, a member of the congregation suggested I might bend my mind to the modernization of Christianity. It was a kindly, well-intentioned suggestion, but I am not sure that modernization ought to be carried out, or even, indeed, that it can be done at all. How does one go about devising an 'up-date' of the story of Christmas or the narrative of the Passion? One tries, of course, to find ways of restating old truths, but that is hardly modernization. And yet I am aware that a number of people feel that Christianity as traditionally understood is inadequate. I am going to mention one or two of the ways it is thought to be inadequate, though I do so mainly to show why the idea of modernization seems to me problematic, even perhaps irrelevant.

The first and most obvious respect in which Christianity may be judged inadequate is as a form of technology. Perhaps this is because we sometimes pray as though we could inject a distinct and separate spiritual variable within a technical problem. I mean that when you are flying in a dodgy plane over the Atlantic, prayers do not affect a problem which derives from the principles of aero-dynamics and can be traced to faulty servicing.

My eldest son once put it to me economically, perhaps even brutally: 'Christianity doesn't *do* anything.' Confronted by a car which will not move the last thing you need is more Christianity. It is no good blessing it like a priest or cursing it like Basil Fawlty. Cars, like planes, belong to a world of technical cause and effect quite distinct from the world of benedictions, consecrations, prayers, and acts of faith and love.

Put like that it is quite clear that nobody supposes Christianity to be some variety of cause-effect mechanism. And, equally, nobody really supposes that some form of technical up-date can nobody really supposes that some form of technical up-date can be devised for it. It has not yet been suggested that we replace our scriptures by engine maintenance manuals or convert cathedrals into garages and vestments into overalls. We know a 'category mistake' and this is a very obvious one. Christianity is *not* a kind of failed technicality. (If it were you couldn't trust the world. You would never know whether someone was tinkering it about with their prayer.)

The second respect in which Christianity is sometimes judged inadequate is with regard to the running of modern society. Certainly a practical politician will not consult the Bible for help on the details of budgetary policy. Holy Writ does not deal with the public sector borrowing requirement. And people frequently say that we need to mint new morals to deal with new social situations. So the Bible is judged deficient both technically as economics and - more importantly - archaic as a moral guide.

The point may be made by a current example. Professor A.M. Halsey is a Christian and he helped frame the recent Report on the inner city. Unemployment and urban dereliction are, in his view, inconsistent with the Christian duty of good neighbourliness. Professor Bryan Griffiths is also a Christian and personal adviser to Mrs Thatcher. He believes that inflation is a form of unacknowledged theft which robs those without industrial muscle, above all, the elderly. Both of these men know that the Bible is entirely premodern *in so far as* it has nothing to say about the effect of the supply of money on the performance of the economy. It doesn't even attempt to enter into the moral problem of inflation as an alternative to unemployment. But - as we are all perfectly aware - that doesn't imply some need for modernization or suggest we need to devise new moral standards. Christianity offers us principles, pictures of perfection, and embodiments of goodness to reflect upon; and it affirms fundamentals not to be disregarded. Justice, love, peace and reconciliation never become archaic. As to specifics and technicalities, we are free to use our minds; and we are also morally free to direct our wills and our hearts.

There is a third respect in which Christianity is sometimes

judged in need of modernization. The world, as pictured by faith, seems wildly out of line - *out of scale* you may say - with a cosmos originating in the Big Bang and constantly expanding. Theology needs a radical adjustment to modern cosmology.

Yet that is a dangerous half-truth. For one thing, a faith which simply reflects scientific knowledge is not faith and, in any case, rapidly shares in the obsolescence of our scientific understanding. Just over a hundred years ago, Herbert Spencer published his 'Principles' which offered a most impressive synthesis of what was then known. But if Christianity had adjusted to Herbert Spencer it would by now be nothing but by-gone science. Of course, much could have been learnt from those 'Principles', for example, Herbert Spencer's refusal to separate material and spiritual as rival and separate principles. But modernization in the scientific style of 1884 would have been fatal.

Why? Surely, someone will say, it is at least obvious that Christianity is ridiculously out of scale. But we are not comparing like with like. Science works on a mathematical scale and Christianity works on a scale of value or worth. The physical world has to do with extension, with dimension, perhaps, one might say with the infinite addition of further noughts. The noughts, however impressive, *signify* nothing. But within the scale of life, faith affirms the singular and the human: every single one to *count* infinitely. It sees the heart of the *matter* in flesh and blood. You can deny that scale. What you cannot do is to *modernize* it. Faith says that mere immensity on its own doesn't count. It can't count and it doesn't; human beings can count and they do.

Within the stupendous panorama of creation there has emerged a counting, speaking creature who can himself create infinitely expanding words of meaning through sign, word, picture, and gesture. This creature, because he is speaker and maker of pictures and signs is also narrator, reciter, and the teller of his own story. No other being tells its story, creating history, remembering, storing, and *re*-creating *history*.

Christianity belongs not to the world of shifting techniques or accounts of cosmic evolution. It belongs to that flesh and blood world of word, gesture, sign, and story. Its elements are the word, the gesture, the sign and the narrative. What else do we do in Church on Sunday morning but sign, narrate, and commermorate? The signs we make are of birth and of death, of giving and receiving. And the story we tell has at its centre - its crux - the giving of flesh and blood itself, the most precious thing in the world, the offering of the whole person. The fundamental act in the drama is the transformation of flesh and blood in the moment of birth - of incarnation - and at the point of sacrificial death: vulnerable child and desperately wounded man. The signs we make join birth and death, Christmas and Easter together: one feast, one offering, the Word made flesh, Emmanuel, God with us.

The Baptism.
The Transition

'And the Lord said, Arise, anoint him for this is he.'
I Samuel 16:12

'Then cometh Jesus from Galilee to Jordan unto John to be baptized of him.'
St. Matthew 3:13

Let us consider the meaning of baptism. To do that we have to look at these two linked texts and think a little about how the Church from the time of the writers of the New Testament till today has interpreted and used sacred scripture. In one way it is all quite simple. The Church as it meditates on a sacred text looks for parallels. Indeed, as the New Testament writers composed their narratives and letters they saw parallels and patterns in the Old Testament which prefigured the events of the New. We, too, look for parallels.

A simple example of this looking for parallels is found in the two texts above. We can see that St. Matthew presents the baptism of Jesus as a moment of *recognition*. As Christ descends into the waters, His divine sonship and His special mission are recognized. 'This is my beloved Son.' We can also see that the writer of the first Book of Samuel is concerned with an act of recognition. Samuel comes to Jesse looking among his sons for a king: he who shall rule over Israel. As the sons pass before him they are each in turn rejected. But then David the shepherd boy appears. Samuel hears a voice recognizing the future king: 'Arise, anoint him, for this is he.'

By looking at these two stories the Church asks us to search for similarities. The more we look the more parallels appear. First, the new king in each case comes from Bethlehem. Then, we notice that David and Jesus are the unlikely ones: God chooses the weak to confound the mighty. David and Jesus are destined to rule Israel and both are shepherds and kings. They each receive a special

26

mark of their mission. David is anointed with oil and Jesus is baptized by water. Oil and water, anointing and baptism, signify a new stage, inaugurating a new Kingdom. The oil inaugurates a temporal Kingdom, the water inaugurates a Kingdom not of this world. So what Samuel and John the Baptist do is an act of *recognition*, marking the beginning of a new era. That is made clear in the two texts:

The Lord tells Samuel: 'For this is He.'

The voice of God at the baptism says: 'This is my Beloved Son.'

Now, of course, we can look at *all* these parallels, but I think we are chiefly drawn to look at *one*, which is the moment of recognition. You could even call it a moment of *confirmation*.

'For this is He.'

'This is my Beloved Son.'

Baptism then, for Christ, and for all Christians, is an act of recognition, and one which confirms and begins a new era in the Kingdom of God.

But the Church meditating on these parallel events in the old dispensation and the new dispensation sees further. Now we can turn our attention away from Samuel's relationship to David and John the Baptist's relationship to Jesus. There is a broader set of parallels to be found, deeper and more powerful. We have to go back to the Captivity of Israel in Egypt and the Crossing of the Red Sea, to Israel's achievement of liberty, the wandering in the wilderness, and the giving of the Law in the Ten Commandments. Here we have a whole series of parallels, each following the other, with the climaxes being a great transition, a crossing-over, a passing through the waters, and the passing of a new law.

The Church thinks of Israel in Egypt as a child, under tutelage. But a time comes to leave this state of tutelage and cross over to a new liberty. So the children of Israel leave Egypt and come to the great moment when they must make the transit of the Red Sea. They pass through the waters and sing a new song of praise for their deliverance, for their new liberty and independence. But now they must face the temptation of the wilderness and wanderings for forty years. As the climax of all this, they will receive a new law and enter into the Kingdom as the heirs of promise. So here we have a vast *pattern*: captivity and tutelage; the moment of transition through the waters; the temptation; the new law and the Promised Land or Kingdom.

The Church meditating on this sequence sees the parallels in the life of Christ. First He is subject to His parents, under tutelage, but '. . . out of Egypt have I called my son'. So Christ, too, comes to the moment of transition which is a passing through the waters. Where the Israelites entered the Red Sea, Christ entered the River Jordan. And as the Israelites wandered forty years, being tempted in the wilderness, so Christ stays forty days in the wilderness, being tempted of the Devil. This leads to a new law and a new Kingdom. Where Moses gives the Ten Commandments, Christ set forth the new commandment of the Kingdom of God. The old Israel entered the Promised Land; the new Israel entered the new age of God's Kingdom.

This, then, gives another meaning of baptism: from subjection to liberty, from old dispensation to new. It is the great moment of *transit*, signified in the crossing of water or immersion in water.

Baptism, then, is recognition, confirmation, and the transition to new laws and new liberties. But that is still only half the story. As the Church looked back at those great crossings of the past, such as the passage of the Red Sea, and the passing of Joshua over Jordan, it thought of the greatest crossing of all: from death to life. We have an example of this in the lesson for Easter day, which is about the crossing of the Red Sea, and the triumphal song of the redeemed on the other side. Christ passes through the waters of death, and brings all His people to light and immortality. We have another example in the great Welsh hymn 'Guide me O thou great Jehovah'. As the hymn puts it:

> When I tread the verge of Jordan,
> Bid my anxious fears subside,
> Death of deaths and hell's destruction,
> Land me safe on Canaan's side.

So here are two crossings of water. First there is our own encounter with the River Jordan, as we stand at the margin of death. Pilgrim passes through the waters to new life, and all the trumpets sound on the other side. But, second, there is our death in Christ, the crucifixion of the old self, in which all the past is washed away, and our resurrection with Him. We experience a death of our old selves, as we are totally immersed, and as we re-emerge in the power of resurrection. There is a new life in this life *and* a new life in Christ beyond the deadly sea of mortality. We have passed through the waters of the Red Sea and the waters of Jordan.

So, as we recapitulate, we see all the meanings of baptism forged into one summary act: recognition and confirmation; the transition to new laws and liberties; the burial of an old self beneath the waters so that we may rise, washed and purified, to a new life; the crossing of the last river, death, to resurrection. This means that the *beginning*, baptism, already speaks of the end: death and resurrection. That is why St. John Damascene says in one great phrase in his Easter hymn:

Our Christ hath *brought us over*
With songs of victory.

That is why St. Paul puts it in one great phrase in his Epistle to the Romans:

Therefore are we buried with him *by baptism unto death*; that
like as Christ was raised up from the dead by the glory of the
Father, even so we also should walk in newness of life.

Baptism is newness of life - life, if you like, in the Spirit. We are baptized not only with water but with fire and the Holy Ghost. We cross by water and by fire. The old spirits are cast out and exorcised; we are fired by a new spirit.

These great transitions or *rites of passage* have just two further elements with which I conclude. Consider the Feast of the Circumcision, in which a male Christ was taken into the local community of Israelites. Circumcision signifies the old Covenant of God with Abraham and with all the children of Israel. But Christian baptism eliminates the difference between male and female, between local nation and the universality of humankind. Circumcision is to Israel; baptism is to all nations, tribes and tongues. Baptism has a universal scope: one Lord, one faith, one baptism, one God and Father of all, who is above all, in all, and through all. So baptism takes us into a universal sonship, joint-heirs with Christ, and with the redeemed of every nation.

And that can be shown by one further parallel: with the earliest layers of the Old Testament. Naturally, it has to do with water. Noah warned of a deluge or judgement by water. But he built an ark into which all creation might come. Here every creature might pass through the forty days of flood until they finally were safe and saved.

Here is the pattern. The prophet warns: the people neglect his warning. An ark is built, the barque of Christ, in which all humankind may be saved from the deluge, along with the whole of creation. And so animals and humankind enter two by two into the ark, crying Alleluia, Alleluia. They have been recognized and confirmed, they have been taken in and washed, they have passed over the sea from captivity and liberty, and they have passed from death to life.

John the Baptist.
The Desert Way

'... Make straight in the desert a highway for our God.'
Isaiah 40:3

St. John the Baptist was the forerunner of Christ and one who pioneered the way of the desert. My theme is the desert, but I want first to scrutinize the Old Testament lesson which goes with the story of John the Baptist. That lesson is about Samson and clearly the people who have compiled the lectionary want us to see in Samson some kind of forerunner of John the Baptist. But how? In what way can Samson lead us toward the strange, ascetic figure of John the Baptist?

To begin with, Samson does not look very promising as a John the Baptist figure. After all, he succumbed to Delilah whereas John the Baptist resisted the blandishments of Salome. Samson seems like a Hebrew version of Hercules, performing mighty labours of valour with the jawbone of an ass. But the lesson we read from the Old Testament is not about these Herculean tasks or about Delilah. It concerns the announcement (you might call it the annunciation) whereby Samson is to be set aside from birth for a special role. In order to perform that role he had to become a Nazarite, and adopt a certain style of life as part of a spiritual preparation. A Nazarite was not allowed to cut his hair or to drink. Clearly in these respects Samson and John the Baptist have much in common. John the Baptist, too, is set aside from birth for a special mission and he adopts the spiritual disciplines which that mission requires. He refuses the delights of eating and drinking and will not wear soft raiment. Samson and John the Baptist are both, after their manner, called from their birth to be ascetics. In different ways they are part of a single tradition.

As we turn to John the Baptist himself, we notice that his special mission in the desert complements the mission of Jesus.

Just as there are parallels between Samson and John the Baptist, so there are differences between John the Baptist and Jesus. John is a man essentially of the desert; his preaching belongs to the desert area round about the Dead Sea. He announces the coming Kingdom by a baptism of water. Jesus, by contrast, is a man of the Galilee, who inaugurates God's Kingdom by a baptism of the Spirit. Jesus enters the wilderness, but *only* for a limited period of forty days.

The two figures complement and contrast with each other above all in their attitude towards the good things of creation. John the Baptist embraces the rigours of asceticism, and resembles the members of the Qumran community - the Dead Sea sect - who constantly purified themselves with water and undertook rigorous exercises to prepare the way of the Lord. Jesus 'came eating and drinking'. The New Testament affirms that the way of the desert *and* the way of the Galilee are *both* forms of wisdom. According to the writer of St. Matthew 'wisdom is justified of her children'. In other words, what is wise *depends* on what is your particular calling and vocation. Interestingly enough, Christianity has developed the special wisdom of rigour more than Judaism. The line that runs through Samson, the Nazarites, the Qumran community and John the Baptist leads straight to the Desert Fathers and Christian monasticism; among the Jews, however, that line almost peters out.

So, in Christianity we have a double wisdom: the wisdom of the desert and the wisdom of the Galilee, the rigour which suspects the good things of creation, and the holiness that accepts and uses them.

What *is* the message from the desert and what do we learn in and from the wilderness? First, of course, we learn the bareness of the self as all the natural and social support systems are stripped away. Chatter recedes, distractions are distanced, timetables are obliterated. What is left is the human spirit in direct confrontation with the Word. The desert is the place where the ineffable name is proclaimed; where the redeemed of the Lord suddenly realize they are walking with a cloud going behind and before.

The wilderness forces men and women to find their inner resources and to make decisions. They have retreated there in order to know themselves and in order to decide. So the wilderness is also the place of temptation, in which delusions and chimeras must be set aside. With the setting aside of delusion goes the proclamation and acceptance of judgement. John the Baptist in the desert erupted with a message of judgement. Once all the props have been removed it becomes possible to judge rightly. So we have the solitariness, the silence, the Word, the testing and temptation, and the judgement.

What is the judgement of the desert? Negatively it is an eruption of rigour against the City of Destruction and against those who are at ease in Zion. It breaks false idols and images, above all the image of the Golden Calf. Individual property and family are challenged in the name of common possessions, of Sister Poverty and Fraternity. Life is not getting and spending and laying waste our human powers. Positively it is the founding of a school of charity, for men and women who are learning to hope in mercy and be merciful. There is a high rare compassion in the desert, which extends even to the animal creation. Monks are friends to lions, seals and birds, as well as to humankind.

Thomas Merton was a monk vowed to silence who chose the wilderness and embraced the school of Sister Poverty and Sister Charity. He saw his vocation as going back in a line leading directly to John the Baptist. He wrote a poem on the contemplative vocation which he called 'The Quickening of St. John the Baptist'.

But we have to realize that the desert is *not* final: it only runs before the Kingdom. The desert is the shadow, necessary to a wider substance. It is part of the journey, which leads by way of wildernesses to promised lands. The lands of promise are not marked by privation but by fullness. The goodness of creation is not in the end to be denied but affirmed: the Kingdom is eating and drinking and the Messianic feast. Beyond the desert is Jerusalem, which is an image of the redeemed city. The Bible contains three spiritual terrains: the wilderness, the paradisal garden, and the city - the city which is destroyed, like Sodom and Babylon, and which also comes down from heaven adorned as a bride. The necessary journey through the wilderness, the difficult and testing sojourn in the desert, is *en route*: to the rose, the garden, the vineyard, the stream in the midst of the heavenly city. The wilderness abuts the garden of Paradise; the straight journey in the desert points towards - towards what? - towards the moment of attention and epiphany, when 'the time of the singing of birds is come'.

Quinquagesima.
The Way of Love

'Though I speak with tongues of men and of angels and have not
charity, I am become as sounding brass or a tinkling cymbal.'
I Corinthians 13:1

'As the apple tree among the trees of the wood, so is my beloved among
the sons. He brought me to the banqueting house and
his banner over me was love.'
Song of Songs 2 : 4

It is very difficult on Quinquagesima Sunday, especially when it
overlaps the Feast of Bishop Valentine, not to speak about love.
But love, I confess, is not an easy topic, because it is really a
summary of the good and includes all our caring and our cherish-
ing. Love in the deepest sense of Christian charity, includes all
kindness and magnanimity, benevolence and generosity, patience
and self-giving. To speak of love is to speak of that passionate
disposition of our innermost self that issues in virtue.

Love is not only present in that inner disposition. Love goes
out and is found in attachment to the other. It is inner affection and
outer attachment. It concerns all those things which we cherish
and it concerns those persons to whom we cleave. Love originates
within, but goes out to a whole realm of nature and of humankind.
Love is movement - from I to you or from I to the world; to a
pattern or a plant, a sound or a shape, an animal or a place. Once
we love we *tend* and we look after, because we are involved. This
tenderness in us creates a presence which can be felt. We know
what it is to experience the presence of that love. Love in action
is tangible.

The Eucharist itself is a kind of love-in-action because it
makes tangible the presence of love through tokens and pledges.
Holy Communion is the movement of love's tokens as they are
passed from *hand to hand*. It is the giving and receiving of a token
and, therefore, an engagement. To receive those pledges of love is

to acknowledge that at the deepest level we are engaged and bonded. The presence of love brings us together. We know it to be love because it is a giving once and for all, without stint, without money, and without price. Love invests 'the other' with preciousness and discerns an infinite value. Love is actually *made* in the exchange of tokens, and desires nothing but love in return. What passes between human beings *is* love-making, here in the Eucharist - yes - and for that matter in every moment of giving, bonding and engagement. We are creatures strangely and wonderfully made because we are able to *make* love. It is in *what passes between us* that life is actually created and affirmed.

St. Paul in his great hymn to love, goes further and begins to break the bounds of language by speaking of the partial and the complete, the imperfect and the perfect. Love is not only concerned with the creation of life, with engagement, with the affirmation of bonding and attachment, but with intimations of the perfected, the renewed, and the complete. We are, says St. Paul, always living partially and obscurely. But the inner tendency of love is to seek the perfect and the complete: love desires fulfilment. There is in all of us a desire for perfection and for plenitude.

I want to look now into the mysteries of this second theme of St. Paul's hymn: the promise that he finds in love of completion. We most of us know from our own experience that human love leaves as many stricken as it leaves fulfilled. The tally of human love is often disappointment and a sense of mismatched aims. So, how do we approach this promise of fulfilment through love and of face-to-face encounter? Do we now sharply separate divine love from creaturely love and say that only in divine love are the promises kept and the desires fulfilled? That indeed, is the answer given in much Christian thought and experience: the earthly is not as the heavenly. Perhaps, indeed, there is little or no commerce between them at all. But in my account of Communion, I made them complementary. I ran one alongside the other, speaking of the making of love through pledges and tokens passed from hand to hand, through engaging ourselves, through gifts and offerings. I took the path of mystical theology by placing the divinely

creative and the humanly pro-creative adjacent one to the other.
I am following the current of mystical theology in supposing that
the erotic and the mystical interpenetrate, so that divine love and
human love feed in the same pastures and draw from the same
well.

Think, for a concluding moment, of the images and sights
which affect us most deeply and stir us to delight. Think of wells
and rivers, think of the fountain, think of the tree, and think of the
sun. In summoning up those images you have recalled our human
vision of earthly paradise. Such icons fascinate, draw, and attract.
They satisfy and they offer 'quiet consummation'. But they are also
the images which cluster together in the closing passages of
scripture as signs and emblems of fulfilment. There, in John's final
vision, is the healing tree and the never failing fountain: archetypes
of abundant and everlasting life. The fountain rises up for ever,
turning on itself like an eternal ring, describing perfect arcs and
continually replenishing the earth. The tree comes from the fertile
seed and emerges organically. It breaks and it buds. As we
contemplate river and fountain, tree and sun, we encounter and
absorb the emblems of power and renewal; they speak to us at
every level of the source, the energy, the growth, the maturity, and
the consummate power of love. In them we uncover and discover
the emblems of growth and perfection, refreshment and renewal.
As we feed on them in our heart and mind, in our daily experience
of the world, and in the visionary words of sacred scripture, we
undergo an initiation into 'the love that moves the Sun and all the
stars'. They usher the heavenly bridegroom into the secret chambers of the soul and there offer love's banquet.

You perhaps recollect one of the most beautiful of Christmas
carols called 'Jesus Christ the Apple Tree'. What is happening in
that carol to make it so luminous? The carol is from New
Hampshire and the author is meditating on the tree of life in John's
vision and on the image of the apple tree in the 'Song of Songs'. He
writes:

> The tree of life my soul hath seen,
> laden with fruit and always green.

In the Hebrew love song the apple tree is the human beloved, but in the carol the apple tree becomes Christ and He is the eternal source of life and of love. Here, then, is that double meaning which all the visionary signs contain to open the doors of our perception to wonder and to love.

> As the apple tree among the trees of the wood, so is my beloved among the sons. I sat down under his shadow with great delight and his fruit was sweet to my taste. He brought me to the banqueting house, and his banner over me was love.

Lent.
Tests and Angelic Assistance

'. . . and, behold, angels came and ministered unto him.'
St. Matthew 4 :11

The Gallup organization has not yet carried out a random sample to discover what English people believe about angels. If it were to do so the questionnaire might begin something like this:

Q: Do you accept there could be such beings as angels? If your answer is 'Yes' which of the following descriptions corresponds to your idea of an angel? You may tick more than one description. An angel is:

(1) A being of mighty intelligence in perfect harmony with God's will.

(2) A sort of divine power which is capable of falling away from God and wreaking havoc in the world.

(3) A real person, Michael, Gabriel or whatever. Such persons may appear singly, or in a choir or in an orchestra with harps and trumpets.

(4) A way scripture uses of talking about being helpful, or ministered to, or seeing something revealed.

By now you probably feel that some polls are almost impossible to answer.

All the same it *is* interesting to find out what ideas about angels people have, tucked away up there in the mental loft. It would be reasonable to ask them to unpack those unexamined mental pictures for us to have a look. And there the pictures would be. Angels are . . . beautiful creatures, winged, majestic and intelligent, but neither male nor female. They watch over us waking and guard us sleeping. An angel isn't bounded by time or space. Angels appear just before something really big is about to happen and usher in the final judgement, probably from a hill-top. Angels gather rank upon rank, sloping up in a great chain of beings to God.

As these pictures are put on show, the sceptic might say that angels are obviously so much celestial stage machinery. And he would be supported in that by the fact that modern people don't claim to 'see' angels. After all, they claim to see all sorts of other things: fairies, ghosts, UFOs, even winking statues. But if you were running a phone-in and asked people to ring up if they had entertained an angel or seen an angelic squadron in the sky you would land yourself with a pretty short programme. Angels are not even contentious. The Bishop of Durham hasn't denied their existence, and conservative evangelicals have not claimed that on the contrary several have recently been sighted in Hemel Hempstead.

If we are to think seriously about angels, let us see how they enter the sacred narrative of the Bible and how they are presented by the sacred writers. The word 'angel' means 'messenger'; and so we have our basic clue. When an angel appears in the story of our redemption we know that something is about to be revealed, uncovered, set in motion, brought to birth or to final fruition. Angels will be there when great things are begun or finished. They will also signal God's presence in tenderness of supporting grace, or in plenitude of glory.

Just run through the examples. In the story of Jacob the angels ascend and descend the ladder between heaven and earth. In one of the stories of Elijah - one that runs parallel to the temptation of Jesus - they give him new courage to journey through the wilderness and minister to him with food as he sleeps under the juniper tree. In the great vision of Isaiah the angels proclaim God's glory crying 'Holy, Holy, Holy'.

At the beginning of the New Testament the angel of the Annunciation tells the Blessed Virgin of the holy thing which is to be born of her; at the birth of Jesus the angelic choir is composed of messengers of peace on earth. At the moment of Christ's supreme testing in the wilderness, angels come and minister to Him; at the moment of supreme testing in the Garden the Angel of the Agony strengthens Him. It is the angels who carry the message: 'He is not here: He is risen'. And then at the final consummation the angel sounds the Last Trump.

As we scan these different incursions of angels in the Bible, we begin to see what they truly mean. Angels are there at the great crises. They are spiritual agencies of God's presence. They signal a commerce between heaven and earth, as *messengers* and as *ministers*.

One of those great crises is the time of the test and of the wilderness. It is something we all of us enter with foreboding and fear: 'Do not bring us to the test'; 'Lead us not into temptation'. Our spirits fail us at the thought of the wilderness, for we know it is there; we are on trial, faced by chaos and emptiness, tempted to despair, seduced by phantoms of evil.

We, when we enter Lent, confront the wilderness: the journey and the crisis faced by Elijah and by Christ Himself. That journey into the wild and terrible place is universal. We walk forward in our solitariness, asking ourselves who we are and whom we serve and whether grace will really be sufficient for us. The forty days bring out the emptiness of the hole at the centre of our lives; the forty nights are full of their own terror. In those days and nights we are being made, forged, by looking into the bottomless pit and facing the formless waste. We come to *be* through the temptation to find the magical solution, to look for the easy miracle, to succumb to the false ambition and aggrandizement. In this crucible of heat by day and chill by night, we are forced to find ourselves, with all the familiar landmarks and everyday pathways - gone.

And it is somewhere *there* that the heavenly presences we cannot see and barely believe in can make themselves known. Something unfolds, the deepest layer of calm is exposed, the wells of hope are drawn upon. Somewhere in that desert we are touched by ministers of grace - and, as in an infinite mystery - feed on the bread of angels.

Passion Sunday.
Priestly Victim

'... Christ ... an high priest of good things to come ... and ...
mediator of the new testament ...'.
Hebrews 9:11 and 15

In the epistle for Passion Sunday so much is compressed in a few
sentences that Cranmer gave up writing a collect for it and
reduced his prayer to two or three lines. Bishop Patrick tried again
in 1679 and only managed to solve the problem by writing a
prayer which went on for ever. We today are no better placed and
can only really make sense of this language by reading the whole
epistle to the Hebrews. Even when we have done that, we still have
to ask what this dense and powerful argument can mean for us
sixty generations after the event.

Let me try to summarize the epistle to the Hebrews in a
couple of paragraphs. To do that I am going to use the writer's own
ancient technique. It is 'typology' and it involves putting representative ideas and representative people in contrasting columns to
bring out the similarities and the differences. For the writer to the
Hebrews, the central contrast is between two types (or two figures,
if you prefer). There is Moses, who *pre*-figures Christ; and there is
Christ who completes Moses, but who also breaks through to
something new - the New Testament. The idea to hold on to here
is the idea of *breakthrough*, or *opening up*, or *passing into*.

That figurative contrast is complemented by another, this
time between Levi and Christ. Levi stands for priesthood in the old
and limited order, and Christ stands for a universal priesthood
opened up to all the sons and daughters of men. You will notice
that we have already located the two key elements in our text:
Christ who mediates and breaks through to a New Testament, and
Christ who is the high priest of 'all good things to come', including
a shared priesthood of all believers. He opens up the holy of holies
to us all; and that is why the communion service in the Alternative

Service Book opens with the words, also from the epistle to the Hebrews: 'Seeing we have a great high priest, who has passed into the heavens, Jesus the son of God'.

We can now assemble the supporting contrasts quite rapidly till we have almost the complete set of 'types'. First, the old priesthood in the Old Testament offered sacrifices through the blood of animals, *but* our New Testament and our new priesthood is the self-offering of a person who gives his life-blood for all. Second, those old sacrifices conformed to an outward ordinance *but* what we now celebrate is a costly gift of the heart and the inner life. Third, all those sacrifices were imperfect and, therefore, repeated, *whereas* the sacrifice of Christ is perfected once for all and for ever.

And all these changes, says the writer to the Hebrews, take us from the outward to the inward, from a local and material temple to a universal and spiritual one, from mere sign to that which is signified, from shadow to substance, from law to grace, from Sinai to Zion, from Moses to Christ, from dead works to living service, and through death to life eternal.

I think all these transitions or breakthroughs make good sense to us today. We understand well enough what it is to pass from outward observance to inner dedication, from local and visible to universal and invisible, and from the offer of mere things to pure self-giving. Perhaps, in putting it that way, we modernize a little but we still follow the spirit of the text.

Yet, in fact, we are only part way to the central mystery around which all these contrasts turn. At the centre is the high priest who is also the victim and who, through the offering of his life-blood, *breaks through* the veil and takes all humankind into the holy of holies. The son of man, embodying a love which is truly divine, and a spirit which is truly holy, passes into the heavens and enables every one of us to come face to face with God. By his passionate giving the barriers are broken down, between divine and human, and God's real presence made manifest among humankind. The divine life is poured out *for* us and freely given *to* us. We come alive in God and know the joys of heaven.

What the writer of the epistle to the Hebrews has done is to set out all the elements which are at stake in the Passion of Christ, and show that they belong not just to the movement from Sinai to Zion, but pertain to the universal drama of our passage from death to life, and our breakthrough into heaven. This is the argument for a heaven stormed by love.

On Passion Sunday we stand at the symbolic recommencement of all these great transitions. The last battle is a passage of arms between the power of love-unto-death and every device of the power of evil. The Royal banners now quietly assemble around the kingly servant and the priestly victim. He is the high priest of all the good things to come but their coming will enact 'not less than everything'. The costing is and will become the insatiable demand for blood.

Before us now, in the Passion of Christ, is the crisis of our universal human condition. That condition is governed by a law of the spirit which requires that He who feeds the world must do so with His own body and blood. Only through this generous spilling and brimming over of life can the love of God become manifest to us and we be taken up into the Presence. As the sacrifice is offered in the wide temple of the world so the veil is broken, and heaven and earth are filled with the majesty of God's glory. It *is* an entrance, a breaking through; or, as the writer to the Hebrews says as he reaches the conclusion of his great argument:

> You are now come to Mount Zion, to the city of the living God, to an innumerable company of angels, to the general assembly and church of the first-born . . . and to Jesus the mediator of the new covenant, and to the blood of sprinkling that speaks better things than the blood of Abel.

Palm Sunday.
The Crux

'. . . even the death of the cross.'
Philippians 2 : 8

The cross - which on Palm Sunday we hold in our hands - is the signature of the Christian faith. You could not have a simpler sign: a vertical line and a horizontal crossbar. The vertical line joins heaven and earth; the horizontal crossbar stretches out to include all humanity. The cross is inclusive. Draw a circle round it and you see it contains the whole cosmos, a complete world. The cross is all-encompassing.

We also know that this cross is a tree - a tree which spans the beginning and end of time and stands at the crux of the human story. In the beginning there was a mysterious tree of the knowledge of good and evil. When man plucked from it he fell. As he tasted choice and evil he began a career as an alien in a hostile world. Paradise was lost and the world was filled with sin, sorrow and death. But the deadly tree was matched by another, whereby paradise was regained. The tree at the beginning was matched by a tree for the healing of the nations. So, the tree changed its sign from negative to positive. The deadly tree in Eden became the tree of life on Calvary. We are all of us grafted on to the life that radiates through that healing tree.

How does that tree radiate life and healing? It does so by a strange law of spiritual exchange. The law is that life rises again as it is freely poured out and poured away. The law reads: life given is life restored. The gift of blood, the blood donation, is the offer of life. Once this law is obeyed everything is reversed. Out of the free gift comes infinite riches; out of the loss comes gain; out of weakness comes power; out of violence peace. Once the cross is embraced all the great negatives become a positive. They obey a new sign.

The new sign brings evil and love *together*. The cross tells us what evil can do; it also tells us what love can do. The sign of the cross is a sum of evil and a sum of love. And with every negation wrought by evil, we see it reversed, and turned round by sovereign grace. It is just as evil begins finally to wreak its will that God's will is done on earth as it is in heaven. They did as they would with Him; He did as He would with them. Even as the spirit of humankind in Christ flickers under pain and nothingness, hatred, contempt, rejection and injustice, the restoration of man in the image of God is being eternally accomplished. As Christ's face is marred so the image of God in man is restored.

This Sunday is about love's advance and love's entry into the last battle. God's representative comes to the gate of the city and to the way of the cross. We know God has His champion in the stricken physician; in the rejected lover; in the imprisoned innocent; in the deserted prince; in the pantomime king. It is an unequal war and Christ will soon be finished. He will be the sacrificial Lamb, scourged, silent and abandoned. Yet hope's defeat will be love's consummation. By His death He will overcome death and bring life and immortality to light. Worthy is the Lamb that was slain to receive honour, glory, and power, for ever and ever, Alleluia. Hosanna in the highest.

Good Friday.
From Black to White

For many people, Christianity is about being good. They understand it as the golden rule: 'Do as you would be done by'. So far, so good. But it is not very far. If Christianity were really about being good then you would expect some reference to that in the creed. But in the creed there is not a word about goodness. I expect quite a lot of churchgoers would feel more at ease with a creed which went something like this:

I believe in God, who is love

in Jesus Christ, who taught us about that love,

in the holy spirit who keeps us in that love,

and in the community of Christians who share love with each other.

That would, indeed, be a religion for all sensible men and women. How odd and strange, then, that the creed ignores it, and says:

who for us men and *for our salvation* came down from heaven

who was crucified also *for us* under the Pontius Pilate.

We are tempted to say this creed is a religion *about* Jesus, rather than the real religion *of* Jesus, which was all to do with loving your enemies, and doing good to them that despitefully use you, walking the extra mile, acting the part of the Good Samaritan. A Christian is the one who visits the prisoners, protects the fatherless, sells his goods and gives them to the poor, who preaches good tidings of peace. (So, indeed, he is: but that is half a gospel.)

If you do take this view about the simple, ethical message of the good and kind teacher, then you may also feel that somebody right at the beginning got it all wrong. And the favourite culprit is St. Paul. Paul it was who turned the religion of doing good into the mystery of salvation and redemption. He invented a religion *about* Jesus which is not Christianity but what Bernard Shaw pilloried as Crosstianity. Crosstianity is a strange business about the divine son placarded on a gibbet, and about the dying, suffering Lamb.

From him, Paul, came all those evangelical words: redemption, salvation, and justification. But there are not only the distortions we have from St. Paul, but the distortions of somebody with an even stronger imagination, St. John the Divine. The religion which is supposed to have so many wise axioms for living the good life becomes a strange and terrible last battle in St. John's 'Revelation'. There we have Aslan: Lion of Judah and Lamb of God. Unreadable stuff, this 'Revelation', except, of course, for the good chapter at the end about the New Jerusalem, coming down from heaven, and promising that all tears will be wiped away from our eyes. What in heaven's name can you make of a writer who speaks of the Lamb as the bridegroom of the heavenly city, or of the Lamb in the midst of the throne, or strangest of all:

Who are these arrayed in white?
These are they which have washed their robes in the blood of
the Lamb.

So many of our pictures of the Lamb come from that final book which could so easily have been left out of scripture, and nearly was. Better far to have ended with St. John's letters: 'little children, love one another', or on the good advice and high moral standards found in St. James. In St. Paul and in the Book of Revelation, there is too much theology, and above all, too much blood: in short, Crosstianity. The Christian imagination has run wild with blood. We may have a *white* Lamb, good and innocent, who is a sign of obedience, but why a dying Lamb? Why this crimson as well as the white? It is all very well to live sacrificially, being full of decent self-sacrifice, but why does everything centre on the final death and passion? Let us have the good life and the perfect example not the redeeming sacrifice. Yet, as we ask for an example and not a bloody sacrifice, we know that the narrative of the Passion takes up nearly half the gospels. We cannot take out the atoning crimson Lamb and leave the white and innocent example. It is the same all the way through the New Testament. St. Paul talks as much as anybody about love and he sets the most excellent gift of charity above all else, but his white goes with his red. Charity yes, sacrificial living yes, but the goodness and the love are twined with the Passion and the death: the dying lamb. St. Paul is full of injunctions, advice and reflections on good works, but you cannot choose the works and cut out the faith. If you do do that, warns St. Paul, you are left - not with goodness - you are left with sin, with the filthy rags of your supposed righteousness, with the law and the condemnation. You think you have cleaned it all up nicely, and that you will be justified by your charitable endeavours. You are left, in fact, with that store of good behaviour of which you hope the recording angel keeps a proper account. You have built up pages of entries on the right side of the balance sheet and *that* takes you into the Lamb's book of life. You are trusting in the white.

But St. Paul will have none of that whiteness. The warp and woof of his gospel is the red and the white; the innocent Lamb who went to the sacrifice, and by whose blood we are made white. Who *are* these in the Lamb's book of life? Who are these dressed all in white? They are those for whom the tally of good deeds offered no justification whatsoever. And this is how we arrive at that great doctrine of justification: 'We do *not* presume to come to this thy table o merciful Lord, trusting in our own righteousness but in thy manifold and great mercies'. Faith, said Paul; faith *alone*, added Luther, treading dangerously, but treading rightly, if by 'faith alone' we mean that we trust not in the tally of our virtues but in the almighty overflow of love and of grace. Grace is the gift, pure, total, and all sufficient. The priest as he raises the final sacrifice of love, pleads only and always and for ever, the sufficiency of grace and the power of the gift.

And that is the doctrine of Christ the Lamb. The Lamb is white, and innocent and obedient. But that innocence is *obedience unto death*: because white, therefore red. And we, who are black are now white because, and only because, of that red. We are white because of what has been poured out. The blood has been poured into the cup and we raise the full cup as our plea. The blood means life, the *vital* element, given without stint, lost totally that we might be found absolutely. John Donne put it this way:

Oh my blacke soul!
... wash thee in Christ's blood, which hath this might
That being red, it dyes red soules to white.

49

Easter: 1.
The Rising Again

'The third day he rose again.'
The Nicene Creed

Whatever else the resurrection means, it signifies that death could not hold Christ. Death had no more dominion. The 'most glorious Lord of Life' had conquered sin and death and hell.

I cannot imagine the resurrection. The Bible tells me nothing whatever of it, apart from the first bare announcement: 'He is not here. He is risen'. Beyond that the record speaks only of the mysterious presence of Christ by a roadside, at a table, in a garden, on the lakeshore and on the mountain top. It is these luminous images alone that speak to me of how Christ's death was 'swallowed up in victory'.

We find the resurrection of Christ and our own hope of eternal life difficult, because any transformation so total beggars our imagination. This replacement of the continuous cycle of birth and death, by birth-death-and-life, appears to lie outside all our experience. As St. Paul rightly says, 'eye hasn't seen and ear hasn't heard'. We live fearfully and anxiously in our little chambers of bone, scalded and distracted with pain. We rejoice and take delight in everything that affirms life, the movements of a small child, the breaking of a bud, the return and the lushness of growth in spring, but these things often lie, still, within the compass of a cycle of birth, maturation, decay and death. The note of sadness creeps 'always in'. Our response to the miracle of life and creativity is poised over the knowledge of mortality. And too easily our mundane sense of the everyday closes us off from the miraculous altogether.

Yet it seems to me that we have implanted in us two profound apprehensions: one of ebb and flow, change and decay, growth and decline; the other of death and resurrection. We know the declining curve that points to extinction, and we know also of 'life and

50

immortality brought to light'. Fitfully we see the world caught in its eternal aspect. There are, then, these two powerful underground streams in the soul, one embedded in the passing and transient, the other quickened with unknown possibilities and burgeoning powers. We never forget we have here only a short and 'tremulous stay' but we are also drawn forward by emblems which are 'big with their secret'.

How, then, do we put our ears to the ground to catch this current of subterranean faith and hope? How do we learn to read the emblems of immortality? Only by paying a new kind of attention and by opening all the doors of perception. We have to let the great organ of the imagination begin to play and make ourselves ready to receive good but unconfirmed news. In short, we need to be open to the gospel, gods-spell, the divine writing. As Emily Dickinson wrote:

> The only news I know
> Is bulletins all day
> From immortality.
> The only shows I see
> Tomorrow and today,
> Perchance Eternity.

Emily Dickinson saw and heard and described herself as like 'some sailor skirting foreign shores'. She was mapping eternity from a short distance all her life, charting the strange emblems which bore the good but unconfirmed news. The emblem might be an odd fork in the road, a gun at sea, bells in a steeple, or 'the colour of a cruising cloud'. It might be a sudden surmise that 'the horses' heads were toward eternity'.

So what we think we cannot imagine we are skirting all the time. We recognize with a start what those emblems can really say: the gun at sea, the bell, the turn of the horses' heads. We begin to recollect a language we have always known, but which comes from beyond our current confinement.

One man who read and wrote this language, almost more clearly than anybody, was a Welsh doctor, Henry Vaughan, who rode around the Brecon Beacons. To him it was a secret spring, or well, or mine, from which he drew constantly. His emblems were fountains and shining stones, above all, stars. He was a poet of light and water and 'the great chime'. He wrote:

> I saw Eternity the other night
> Like a great ring of pure and endless light

He also wrote, 'There is in God, some say, a deep but dazzling darkness'. Light shining from star and from stone conveyed intimations of immortality. The lesser lights of star and stone led him to the eternal source of all light and all seeing.

One of the most powerful modern translators of the emblems all about us was Gerard Manley Hopkins. For him, as for most of us, the stream of despair lay deep, and strangely close to the fountain of life, hope and immortality. He lamented how everything is consumed by death and by distance, 'beat level' by vastness and by time. He described the world around us as a vast bonfire, with every mark of man passing quickly into an unfathomable, enormous dark. Our human spirit, he wrote, is flesh-bound at best, like a skylark trapped in a cage. Yet the trapped bird knows the free fells are there, and it sings. Humankind sings because it still recollects and grasps the language of promise, even as it bows before the cycle of decay and extinction. Humankind, says Hopkins, seems nothing but a poor broken potsherd, mere mortal trash ready for the trash-can, a piece of matchwood, a patch, just a joke. But the matchwood is really 'immortal diamond': the shining stone.

> Across my foundering deck shone
> A beacon, an eternal beam. Flesh fade, and mortal trash
> Fall to the residuary worm;
>
> In a flash, at a trumpet crash,
> I am all at once what Christ is, since he was what I am, and
> This Jack, joke, poor potsherd, patch, matchwood, immortal
>   diamond,
> Is immortal diamond.

Easter: 2.
Communicating

'. . . he was known of them in breaking of bread.'
St. Luke 24:35

Think about the distinctive signs or markers of Christian faith. Every faith has distinctive signs which summarize its meaning, for those who hold it, and for the world outside. For the Christian faith those signs are a cross and a meal. A Christian is someone who walks behind a cross and who eats common meal. At crucial moments many Christians, perhaps the majority make both signs simultaneously: they sign themselves with the cross and stretch out their hands for the meal. Many priests make both signs simultaneously: they make the sign of the cross with the bread as they offer it to the believer. They also make the sign of the cross over the sacred meal. And the bread itself is stamped with a cross. The bread, shaped in a circle to signify the whole redeemed cosmos, carries the stamp of a cross. The Christian then, is not only one who walks behind a cross, and not only one who adopts it as his sign, but one who takes the sign into himself, absorbs it into his own body and blood. There could not be a more fundamental signature than this: to absorb the sign into your own body.

What do these signs mean: the cross and the meal? We know that we make and give these signs to identify ourselves as Christians; and we know that others identify us because we make these things our signature. But what *do* they signify? What are we trying to tell ourselves and tell others by a cross and a meal? What, in short, are we talking about in this extraordinary sign language? Is there a code book which will give us the clue to these movements of the hands: the semaphore of hands which sign the cross in the air and stretch out to receive a gift of bread?

Let me look up the code book of this Christian semaphore - or Christian metaphor if you prefer - and translate the sign. As I turn to the code book, I first look up the cross. Here it is ... '+'. I make the semaphore with my hands and I see that the translation is: death and sacrifice. Then I look up the hand movements of stretching out to receive a gift of bread ...' U'. And I see that the translation is: life, and the presence of God in a gift. So now we have the clues to the sign language. We have the meaning of our acts. The Christian is talking about death and sacrifice; he is talking about new life and a presence realized for ever in a gift. In the simplest possible form: God gave Himself on the cross and gives Himself into our hands for ever. What more beautiful language than this: the language of the eternal gift?

And that, of course, is why we join in a Eucharist. Eucharist means thanksgiving: giving thanks in return for a gift. Anthropologists have a name for it, which is 'the gift relationship'. Am I complicating this? No, it is the simplest possible relationship and the best relationship we humans can engage in - the giving and receiving of gifts. Take, eat; this is my body which is given for you. Here we have the broken body of the cross; here we have the living body of His presence.

One of the most beautiful manifestations of Christ's resurrected presence is found in the story of the disciples on the road to Emmaus. They are confused and uncertain. They do not know that Christ is risen and that Christ is with them. He is already beside them speaking to them. As he joins their company he speaks of death and resurrection. But then he gives them the sign of His presence. He breaks bread and becomes known to them. He identifies Himself in the breaking of bread. At one and the same moment they know the sacrifice and recognize the presence of Christ.

All Christian faith since Easter takes place and is realized by that semaphore. As Christ died and lives, so says the semaphore, you die and live. You are identified *by*, you are identified *with* His cross and His resurrection; you, at one and the same time, are joined in His sacrifice and receive the gift of His presence.

Easter: 3.
Signs of the Breakthrough

'... the mystery of God should be finished ...'
Revelation 10:7

I am going to try to break the Christian code. I shall offer, maybe, a small postscript to scripture, interpreting the signs and tracing the deep structure of hope.

Christianity is, I suggest, a sign language: these things 'shall be a *sign* unto you'. We trace the sign and we translate the code.

The code as I understand it is transmitted in the last supper and in the final sacrifice. That supper and that sacrifice are one and the same last and final act. The common elements in both are breaking and offering. The breaking and the offering constitute a meal. What else do you do at a meal but break and offer, break and offer, break and offer?

To break and to offer is to unite the whole company of the guests who attend the table. The sharing *out* is *in*-corporation in the fraternity. It is an act of inclusion. But no fraternity can be incorporated and constituted without cost. The unity of humankind around the common table has from the very first been broken. The hand of man has turned against the hand of man; all hands are stained with the blood of broken fellowship. So that primal, primaeval breakage has to be reversed, by hands which receive the hurt and bear the cost. The cost of breakage will be borne in the breaking of a body and in the shedding of blood. The code book tells us that 'without the shedding of blood is no redemption', meaning that there can be no recovery, no restitution, no reversal, without the total gift of God's essence and His very self.

So the gift that is proffered and the body which is broken is God in Christ: He is both giver and gift, He who offers up and He who is offered, at once priest and victim. And with the making and the tracing of the sign - the fracture and the offering - He is sacramentally present, made known in the breaking of bread. So we bring together a gift and a presence. The offering is a present; the offering also makes Christ present under and by a sign; and the offering is a re-presentation, or 'representation', of the last acts of Christ at the supper and on the cross. It re-enacts and re-presents; it does *not* repeat what was done 'once for all'.

I have used the word 'enact' and now I will change to the word 'gesture'. The cross and the supper are the divine gesture, evoking in us a response. The sign language asks for a reception. And that is signified and sealed in our reception of the gift. We *ingest* the broken body, and it makes us whole. The breaking has healed the terrible brokenness in ourselves; the fracture of the body of Christ has restored the fracture in our souls and the breakage in our fellowship one with another.

And in so doing it has reversed the law of sin and death, bringing life and immortality to light. As breakage makes whole, so death brings immortality to light. Those who respond to the gesture by ingesting the body of the Lord receive into themselves the medicine of immortality and the resurrection presence. They are united in their risen and triumphant Head, taken with Him into Godhead, made one with the Father. They have communicated with each other and with God: by the making and receiving of sign language and of gestures.

Just as the sign language of 'breaking' reverses and cancels all breakages, in the soul and in the fellowship, so it looks back and forward. It looks back and forward because it stands at the crux, the crossing-point. This is the last feast of an old order and testament, and the first feast of the new order and testament. The law and Moses are cancelled and completed by the grace of Christ. As the old order and Old Testament looked back to the glorious liberation of the whole people of God by Moses from bondage under the sign of blood and of the slaughtered Lamb, so the new order and New Testament is celebrated by a looking forward to a liberation of the whole people of God under the great seal of the Lamb who was slain and who is worthy to receive all honour and blessing. Here we arrive at the conclusion of the great code: the mysterious sign of the Lamb who is in the midst of the throne and who is the sole light of the heavenly city, New Jerusalem. This completes the mystery, and there is no more to be said except 'Amen' and 'Amen'.

I have tried to reuse the language and imagery of the Bible in a concentrated form. I want above all to bring out the meaning of what might otherwise seem a strange ceremony in which we mysteriously take bread and wine and understand it as the body and blood of Christ, and as His presence with us. We call ourselves communicants and I have aimed to show what is being communicated simply by making a slight shift from the theological language of 'sign' to the idea of 'sign language', or crossword, or semaphore, or code. I have achieved a marginal increase in distance, by speaking of the Bible as a 'code book' and of Christianity as the 'great code'. In other words I have deployed the full panoply of Christian language but slightly shifted the field of understanding to the science of reading signs and of breaking codes.

I am also trying to penetrate to the deep structure of hope. That means I have to locate the key elements in what is being said or done, and I do that by appealing to human universals: to division and unification, gift and reception. Everything turns around those mighty oppositions: break, unite; give, receive. The unity of man with man is broken: humankind must once more be in solidarity. The unity of man with God is sundered: God and man must once more be at one. The unity of our souls is severed by sin; we must be inwardly healed and restored. And that reunification demands a cost commensurate with the loss: the brokenness of our condition can only be met by the brokenness of God Himself. His brokenness feeds our brokenness as pure gift. So the great reversals begin: from breakage to unity, from sin to redemption, from death to life. It is all summarized as the broken and slaughtered Lamb takes His place at the centre of the throne and of the heavenly city. At that point the seals themselves are broken, the code has been opened up and, in the words of St. John the Divine, 'The mystery of God is finished'.

Easter: 4.
Dying to Live

'... the Lord hath taken away ...'
Job 1:21

'... if we be dead with Christ, we believe that we shall also
live with him.'
Romans 6:8

I want to take two texts and counterpose them against each other.
The first is found in the Old Testament, chapter 1 of the Book of
Job. After Satan had been allowed to engineer every disaster
against him, Job said:

> Naked came I out of my mother's womb, and naked shall I
> return thither: the Lord gave, the Lord hath taken away;
> blessed be the name of the Lord.

The second text is found in Paul to the Romans, chapter 6:

> If we be dead with Christ, we believe that we shall also live
> with him.

I want to reflect on these two texts, using to some extent, the work
of John Bowker in two important books 'Problems of Suffering in
the Religions of the World' and 'The Religious Imagination and
the Sense of God'.

One of the things that stops us understanding the Old
Testament is the fact that we can read the Bible backwards. When
we focus on any Old Testament text we use lens provided by the
New Testament. The New Testament, of course, speaks of the end
of the story, and so, when we turn to the middle of the story, we
cannot imagine how uncertain is its direction, how veiled and
surprising the conclusion. We think of Jews as Christians who
have been told only half a tale, and we mentally fill in the other half
for them. This is especially true when something crops up in the
early part of the story which seems to suggest the conclusion with
which we Christians are familiar. So, at Christmas, we pick out
bits of the story and read them as lessons telling and *fore*-telling

a tale of the loving purposes of God. When we perform Handel's 'Messiah' we sing 'I know that my Redeemer liveth' as if the writer of the Book of Job had some notion of redemption and immortality.

As a matter of fact, he had no notion whatever of resurrection or immortality. It is all very well for St. Paul to say that if Christ is not risen then we are of all men the most miserable. But for almost all the writers of the Old Testament there was to be no rising again, and they were not particularly miserable. They praised God, and trusted Him, at least intermittently, assuming that death was final. What today's atheist assumes as he stares at a corpse, is precisely what the writers of the Old Testament assumed. *Caput. Finis.* When a person dies we think: he won't wake tomorrow, nor May next year, nor sometime in 2053, nor even before the expanding universe contracts and the stars fall back into the originating atom.

We can almost envy nature: the cycle of birth and death and birth continues. Spring comes back, rich with continuity. We in our selfhood don't: the place 'knoweth us no more'. Job thought exactly that: 'For there is hope of a tree, if it be cut down, that it will sprout again . . . [but] Man lieth down and riseth not: till the heavens be no more, they shall not awake, nor be raised out of their sleep . . . thou destroyest the hope of man'.

God, the destroyer. When Job says 'Blessed be the name of the Lord' he sees no hope whatever. Keeping faith for him doesn't and cannot look forward, crying 'And I look for the resurrection of the dead'. He holds to God while having hope 'only in this life'.

But that extraordinary faith is very important for us. The atheist says: this strange attitude of religious trust is only the reflex of fear because men hope against hope that they won't have to die for ever. It is nothing, they say, but a protest against the word 'Never'. Looking at the whole of the Old Testament we can, at least, be assured *that* argument is false. Faith in a relationship with God as expressed in Isaiah or the Psalmists or Jonah has nothing whatsoever to do with compensation or life hereafter. Job says: I know there is *nothing*, blessed be the name of the Lord. Death is *final,* says the Psalmist, 'yet will I trust in Him'.

That is something we too can understand, because we can take away the lens of the New Testament. Take it away and the ancient Jewish relationship to 'God' becomes comprehensible. We come naked, we go naked, but in between one nakedness and another there is something precious in every moment, a transcendent presence in the fabric of the world. That is how things *are*: our sense of fairness, of justice, our desire to stick around for ever just does not arise. 'The Lord gave; the Lord taketh away.'

That doesn't mean to say, of course, that the Jews were content to knuckle under to the way that highest wisdom had disposed things. Job's wife spoke for a lot of them when she told Job to 'Curse God and die'. We know the modern equivalent of that. 'Alright, Deity, you win *if* you are there. Much good your existence does me. You've mishandled the creation badly; I'm not going to worship the celestial inventor of this hopeless torture-chamber. I judge *you*, not the other way round.' 'Curse God, and die.'

The Jews scrabbled around to make sense of two things which appeared certain: first, 'underneath and round about are the everlasting arms'; but second, in the words of Ecclesiastes '[man has] nothing to take with him after all his efforts'. One way was to suppose that at least in this life the just man would be rewarded. At the end of the story of Job, he gets back everything he has lost. In the end, faith and honesty are the best policy - on earth. 'So the Lord blessed the latter end of Job more than his beginning ...'. But we know well enough that that is a cheat; some people even think that part of the book was stuck on to make things happy ever after, instead of leaving everything mysterious.

Another answer, which is almost the same, blames the misfortune on something we've done. People still say, 'What have I done for this to happen to me?' One of the wretched comforters puts this idea to Job: 'Remember, I pray thee, who ever perished being innocent? Or where ever were the righteous cut off?' But the writer of the story has already seen that one coming. He sets Job up, quite artificially, as just the kind of person that argument could not apply to. In the very first verse he makes it plain:

> There was a man in the Land of Oz, whose name was Job; and
> that man was perfect and upright . . .

Yet another answer which the Old Testament gave, and which the rabbis taught, is that we are being tried and tested in a fire, so that we may emerge as true gold without dross. Well, no doubt, some sort of truth lies here. Clearly we do not grow without constantly being tested and testing ourselves; there is no experience of the positive which does not depend on seeing also the chasm of nothingness; life and beauty are created in a womb of darkness and suffering; when the support systems go it is the moment, perhaps the only moment for sure, when we truly ask: what is life *really* about? who am I? what is *ultimately* worthwhile?

That perhaps is part of the truth, but it cannot be the whole truth. The enigma of God's goodness and man's wretchedness - like Job his home destroyed, possessions gone, children killed, health wrecked - remains. God may talk marvellously about His power in creating Orion and the Pleiades, but He gives no explanation.

In the end there are two possibilities for faith, one Jewish, the other Christian. The first is represented by the idea that whatever happens to an individual human being, God's faithfulness will finally restore the community of the chosen and the redeemed. Jerusalem *will* be builded here. Moses sees the Promised Land, even though he himself cannot enter. That is most nobly exemplified in Rabbi Akiba in the moment when Jerusalem was finally destroyed by the Romans in 135 AD. He was being tortured and teased by the Roman Turnus Rufus: Rabbi Akiba replied to his torturer, that at this moment, and only now was he able to love God with all his soul. So he could recite the Shema Israel, fully, for the first time. Shema Israel [*adonai eloheynu adonai ehad*]. Hear o Israel, the Lord our God; the Lord is one.' In death he saw the city and the community, Jerusalem and the Promised Land, liberated, restored.

There is that too in Christianity - 'and I John saw the holy city, new Jerusalem, coming down from God out of heaven . . .' And he that sat upon the throne said 'Behold I make all things new'. But

61

if justice is to be done, then somehow it has to work back through the whole of creation. We have to say, letting partial hope and total disbelief lie in our minds, how they will: 'All we have dreamed of and hoped for of good will exist'. I cannot say, yes, simply I believe it. We are all subject to meaninglessness and hopelessness; and we can only go so far. It is important, perhaps only to be *aligned* with it, or to *allow* it.

We have no idea what mystery lies behind that, but Augustine can tell us what hope it stands for:

> O my soul, wearied at last with emptiness, commit to Truth's keeping whatever Truth has given you, and you shall not lose any; and what is decayed in you shall be made clean, and what is sick shall be made well, and what is transient shall be reshaped and made new and established in you with firmness . . . before God who stands and abides for ever. Amen.

Easter: 5.
Bulletins of Immortality

'And death shall have no dominion.'
Dylan Thomas (taken from Romans 6:9)

The Christian religion teaches us that we are cracked vessels marked for mortality. It also teaches us that we are strangely and wonderfully made. When we concern ourselves with the resurrection we have to think about just *how* strange and how wonderful this cracked vessel really is. The first point then at resurrection time is to establish the crowning miracle of our human existence in this incredible world. There is nothing at all more astonishing and unlikely in the whole of the created order from the structure of DNA to the black holes of outer space than our own specific, individual conscious existence. We are the supreme oddity, the ultimate and most marvellous quirk of the whole fantastic scenario from Big Bang to Megadeath. Let us at least get this absolutely clear to our*selves*, because there is nothing else in the whole universe capable of denying it, let alone affirming it. This is our privilege and ours alone to doubt and suspect who we are and what we portend.

So we have to begin by some sense of our own place in the amazing scheme of things: not as some insignificant speck of irritable dust but as the one crowning glory which *alone*, who *alone*, is able to know what significance is and is able to ask what it all signifies. Here we stand at the intersection of all the worlds, between macrocosm and microcosm, at the gathering point, the central intelligence *agency*, of all the systems of communication there are or ever were. 'There's glory for you.' It is absurd but you had better believe it: all else is contained in you, and you only can make - and remake - something of it.

So what do we make of it? We can, of course, just inspect and dissect, recording and analysing the natural world as mechanism

63

and as organism, recording and analysing the social world as sets of processes and relations. We can act in our capacity as knowers, literally as scientists. The world about us, nature as stone and star and as growth, society as the teeming billions of mysterious others: that world is just an object of enquiry. But our quivering needle of consciousness need not remain in that particular and restricted wave band: it can shift and begin to take in the world in its wholeness. And when we do that the world of nature and of people begins to present itself, nor just as objects and subjects, but as intimation and as emblem. Almost you might say that we become tuned to the world as *heraldry*. What does it herald, what does it intimate? All day and everyday, wrote Emily Dickinson, we take in 'bulletins of immortality'. Our central intelligence agency is infiltrated with hints of the peaceable Kingdom, and with a heraldry of lions and lambs, and a child playing on the hole of the asp. It is impossible completely to shut out this peculiar intelligence, even though we are bound to doubt it and may even resolutely discount it.

So then, you may say, what is this peculiar intelligence that comes through emblem and intimation? How do we decode the reports, unscramble the bulletins? I have no answer to that. I do not have an unambiguous code book which will turn these emblems into clear and indisputable messages. That is not the way this wave band works. There is no indisputable, utterly clear, unequivocal code book on this wave band, though sometimes we pick up a pulsation so clear and so exuberant you think for a moment you know exactly and without doubt what is being intimated and talked about. William Golding once said on television that sometimes in moments of exuberance he knows he is acting in the image of the Maker: the rest of the time he just goes on writing his novels and going about his business. The important point is to keep the wave band open and to be awake and alert to the messages.

In what remains I simply want to be awake on this particular wave length, and to pay attention to the bulletins. I want to be attentive to just two messages: one from the world of things, one from the world of people. The first message, from the world of things, is conveyed by a jet of water, a fountain. On the scientific wave band this is no more than what happens when H_2O is thrust through a pinched aperture. But once picked up on the wave band of emblem, intimation and heraldry, it is a sunburst of glory. The very word 'water' comes from the Arabic for lustre and splendour, especially the transparency of the finest jewels - jewels of the first water.

So for centuries this simple device for manipulating water and thrusting it upward has been picked up as one of the supreme emblems of the perfect. When that which is perfect is come that which is imperfect is done away. A fountain stands for, or rather moves for, and *is*, perfection. We are able to image and imagine the perfect. The dark glasses we usually wear are discarded and we are face to face with something which is simultaneous rest and movement, always changing, always the same, ever new and ever old. The fountain *expresses* power and it *contains* light. A fountain is the exuberant play of fundamental elements: light and water, issuing without interruption from a single point of divine origin.

My second message comes through a quite different kind of movement: the movement of people. Just as water makes its exit and surges *upward* so people can make an exodus and surge *forward*, drawn by promise and anticipation. Let me explain. Just before this Easter pictures appeared on television of vast numbers of people assembling and moving in the city of Budapest. It was a procession of people holding candles, the light thrown upward on their shadowy faces. It was a sort of analogue in the open air of all the peaceful processions held inside sacred buildings and holy houses. That peace march in Budapest was a version of everything that is meant by Palm Sunday: a movement of people making an exodus from the old order and drawn by the prospect of reclaiming the city. The heraldry of that vast human procession was very ancient and completely contemporary. It is 'Resurgam': I will rise again. It is aligned with all the age-old prophecies about caravans of wayfarers eventually entering in at the gate of the Great City. I say 'aligned with' because these movements of people can go dreadfully wrong. They are not, *not* the peaceable kingdom, because they can easily attempt to set up the kingdom by violence. They have the potential for terrible violence in them, for violations as well as for marvellous promise. Yet the forward movement of people is a statement of intent and an intimation of hope. The moving candles speak of resurgence and hope born again.

Of course, looking at the upward movement of water and the forward movement of people does not give us unequivocal messages of hope. Hope and despair, death and life, beauty and desolation, all lie together. As Bela Bartok said, it is life and death, life and death 'down to the very core'. Everything is edged with negation and hedged with dubiety. Yet this rising up and this rising again is a message sent out not only from the natural world of things and from the social world, but a message touching on our very selves, standing as we do at the intersection of all that is. We know the extraordinary fragility *and* the extraordinary miracle of human being. We who pick up the intimations of movement upward and forward, who recognize the perfection of the fountain and are drawn into the procession to reclaim the city, sense also in ourselves, a kind of flow and a kind of movement towards the gate of the city of the Great King.

As Bunyan's Pilgrim felt the forward pull of his journey, the question was put to him by an Evangelist, 'Do you see yonder wicket gate?' He answered, 'No.' Just *No*. He knew the power of the negative. But then the Evangelist said to him, 'Do you see yonder shining light?' He said, '*I think I do*.' Then said the Evangelist, 'Keep that light in your eye, and go directly thereto, so shalt thou then see the Gate . . .' That is the message of Easter.

Keep that light in your eye,
and go directly thereto,
So shalt thou see the Gate.

Bring us, O Lord God, at our last awakening into the house and gate of heaven, to enter into that gate and dwell in that house . . . in the habitation of thy glory and dominion, world without end, Amen.

Ascensiontide: 1.
Glorification

'O God the King of Glory . . . exalt us unto the same place whither our Saviour Christ is gone before.'
Collect for the Sunday after Ascension (Book of Common Prayer)

Ascension, said St. Augustine, is the culminating feast time of the year. There is one word, one only that can fit Ascensiontide. That word is 'glory'. We are now in the feast time of glory. 'Lift up your head O ye gates and be ye lift up ye everlasting doors and the King of *Glory* shall come in.' So, too, our collect: 'O God the King of *Glory*'. So, too, the climax of the *Te Deum*: 'Thou art the King of Glory O Christ . . . when thou hadst overcome the sharpness thou didst open the Kingdom of Heaven to all believers'. This is the feast time of acclamation: 'God is gone up with a merry noise and the Lord with the sound of the trumpet'. *Rex Gloriae*: King of Glory, King of Peace, a title and a name above every name. *There's* glory for you.

With that note of glorification goes the note of exaltation. Exaltation means 'to raise up' and this ascent is not only the ascent of Christ but the ascent of man. Why else should the collect pray the King to *exalt us*? I use the phrase 'the ascent of man' because it is the title of a book on human evolution. Today marks not only the conclusion of the gospel narrative but the conclusion of a stage in human evolution. It is possible to see one aspect of evolution as the development of man from his first animation as a living soul, through stirrings, searchings, spiritual journeyings and climbings, to this last ascent to the face of God. And, of course, there is a cloud surrounding the last ascent. It is the luminous cloud which *must* veil the face of God. Within that cloud lies the peak of being into which Christ has entered, and into which mankind itself has passed and will pass. A cloud around the Most High signifies - in Bible language - the gap which must remain between mortal sight and the blaze of glory.

So what we are saying, as we speak of Christ's journey into that cloud, is that the path to glory has been opened and pioneered. Man has made the final ascent and planted his flag in the highest place. And the representative of our race who has planted the human flag on the peak of being is a scarred, scourged and wounded man. The flag there is the emblem of the Lamb.

Christ entered into *glory*. He made the passage from death to life, breaking all the barriers of mortality. Man in all his searchings and graspings had been confused, held back by space and time. Christ's ascension is not some extraordinary feat of levitation *in* space but a triumph *over* space and time. Christ as representative man, indeed our representative in the holy place, is freed from space and time - in *order* - as St. Paul says, 'that He may fill all things'. In doing so, he re-forms us as 'new creatures'. Evolution is about the 'new creature', the mutant which after ages suddenly emerges. 'If any man be in Christ he is a new creature.' We can be even more daring and take a step directly into the mystery of the Triune God. Man in Christ is a new creature because he is reunited with his Creator, taking a giant leap to the true ground of his being.

Of course, this is high imagery, speaking of cloud and peak, height and ascension, but how else should we speak of the Most High? We are not engaging in some kind of exalted liturgical talk, but trying to envisage a process which is being worked out on a vast scale. The low, shuffling, prehensile creature, shambling through aeons of time towards something always beyond his grasp, reaches a vantage point from which he stretches out and claims the crown. As Wesley puts it: 'Bold I approach the eternal throne, and claim the crown through Christ my own.' Man, the confused and fearful alien, separated by a chasm from the mysterious and unknown Godhead, is suddenly transported - no longer alien but at home, the Son received into the bosom of the Father. No wonder we say at one and the same time 'O God, the King of Glory'; and 'exalt us, exalt us unto the same place'.

But this new stage, which concludes the story of our redemption and our reunification with God, is a beginning as well as an end. The new man, the new creature 'in Christ', is to be agent of a kingdom which restores the whole cosmos. Once this moment in spiritual evolution is achieved, the new man is to bring all things into subjection under His feet. We are, therefore, at the axis between the movement from alien to son, and the movement towards a redemption and restoration of the difficult, resistant stuff of our whole world. The gate of heaven has been opened: what remains is for a kingdom to come on earth as it is in heaven. The breakthrough into the high places and all the life of God is secure, but there remains a vast prospect in which the Kingdom is engaged in deadly, perverse battle.

How, then, can we speak about the coming of the Kingdom? It has been difficult enough talking about the taking of manhood into God using all the imagery of height, ascension and exaltation. We can only make *sign language* about the Kingdom. The Eucharist is simply our sign language about altering the elements of our world. Here we have beggarly elements: raw, resistant materials. We take them up, in the form of bread and wine, and use them as signs of a kingdom. As we raise *up* the elements of bread and wine, we consecrate the substance of our world, as a hint and a foretaste of a new and different order.

Think of what happens as the tiny round element of bread is charged and changed into an emblem of the once and future King and broken to feed all His people. That round element is the whole cosmos in marvellous miniature: macrocosm in microcosm, infinity in a grain of bread. We make a sign with it to show that the entry of the representative man into the high and holy place presages and prefigures His Kingdom and His coming *in glory*.

You will say, perhaps, that in all this I am just translating traditional Christian language about this glorious feast into a crypto-humanism, giving it a gloss of evolutionary terms. Not at all. I am going back to the full-blooded humanism of the Christian religion. Let me remind you, again, of what traditional Christianity actually says. The Athanasian Creed is hardly crypto-humanist but it contains the central affirmation for this feast time: 'not by conversion of Godhead into man, but by the taking of manhood into God.' That is not a reduction but a taking-up. The mystic is just as daring. 'I am as great as God, and He is as little as me.' Of course, it could be blasphemy; it could also be the heart of faith. The Jesuit poet, Gerard Manley Hopkins, ensures it is faith and not blasphemy, profound truth and not crazy egoism.

> In a flash, at a trumpet crash
> I am all *at once* what Christ is, since He was what I am.

Because God became man in all humility, man in all confidence has entered into God.

> O God the King of Glory . . . exalt us, exalt us, exalt us, unto the same place whither our Saviour Christ is gone before, who liveth and reigneth with thee and the Holy Ghost, one God, world without end. Amen.

Ascensiontide: 2.
Exaltation

'Wherefore God also hath highly exalted him . . .'
Philippians 2:9

Some people pass over the ascension in embarrassed silence; others see it as the high point of the Church's year and the pinnacle of Christian rejoicing. Those who see the ascension as a pinnacle often link it directly with the resurrection. He rose; He ascended. *Resurrexit; Ascendit.* Christ's rising and ascending are part of the same movement. In his profound and wonderful commentary on the Mass, Beethoven makes precisely this point. First he states the bare fact of the resurrection starkly and tersely. Then with an enormous thrust the music soars up to the highest heaven, circling round and round in immense spirals of power and praise and joy. Beethoven was not an orthodox Christian, but he grasped the ascension of Christ. For him it was the exaltation of Christ, the representative man, at the right hand of God.

Clearly, we have here to do with the doctrine of Christ and that doctrine is conveyed in pictures. First, we have a Christ who bears the marks of His Passion into the heavenly places: the Christ who wears the diadem is the same Christ who wore the crown of thorns. Second, Christ pleads our cause. The picture language is mysterious here, but the exalted Christ offers Himself, both as the sacrifice and as the great high priest. He *makes* the gift and *is* the gift. Third, He stands before God as the representative man and the Royal head of humankind. Fourth, He breaks down the middle wall of partition, between man and man, man and God. He has 'abolished the enmity'.

All this is summed up in the final images of Christ as Lamb and as Lord. As Lamb He is the sacrifice, marked by suffering and blood. As Lord He is the one who is able to break the seals and open the book of life. The *Te Deum* brings the suffering and the glory together:

71

When thou hadst overcome the sharpness of death
Then didst open the Kingdom of Heaven to all believers.
But if these are the pictures illustrating the doctrine of Christ how
do we translate and interpret them? We have to say, I think, that
all this language is about a *breakthrough*. Humankind in a long
history of many millennia has lost the intimate sense of God's
presence, and the image of God in him is marred and fractured. He
is an alien, separated from nature and from God. But Christ, the
federal head of all humankind, took that marring and fracturing
lovingly into Himself and transformed it. The second Adam bore
the cost of the first.

So human alienation and enmity toward God is costly. There
will be hell to pay; therefore Christ Himself descended into hell. He
knew the absence of God. And it was there, in the deep recesses
of negation and death, that He made captivity captive and brought
life and resurrection to light. By perfect obedience He cancelled
the long tally of disobedience. He broke back into paradise.

As Christ is exalted He takes the human face directly before
God. Previously human beings had pressed toward God by media
and mediations: through priesthoods and prophetic messages. But
in Christ there is *direct access*. When we speak of Christ entering
into the holy place, that entry is made on our behalf. The
representative man is present with God as the Royal head of the
human race, taking our substance into the Godhead. Humanity is
taken into God; the Son is in the bosom of the Father; which is to
say, in other words, that God and man are *at one*.

When the Son is with the Father and humankind in the Son,
then all the divisions and partitions are broken down. Our life is hid
with Christ in God. We are all of one family, one tribe and one
nation. We are neither Jew nor Gentile, male nor female, bond nor
free. The babel of rival languages turns into the common speech
of everybody. A spiritual fire sits on each and every head.

But that, as you know well enough, is the vision. It is what we
celebrate only *by anticipation*. We signal that abolition of the
enmity and the destruction of the middle walls of partition in the
Eucharist. The meal is the anticipation of the universal feast when
all humankind is invited to sit down in the Kingdom. Each

celebration speaks both of the Christ who was dead and is alive for evermore; but it also speaks of the gap that hides from our sight a glory still to be revealed. We look forward, making the sign language of hope and faith. Our signs say that the breakthrough has occurred, but also that the plenitude of glory lies behind a veil. We are separated from Christ by a cloud. St. Peter in his first epistle puts it very beautifully, bringing together both the rejoicing and the distance:

> Wherein ye greatly *rejoice*, though now for a season . . . ye are in *heaviness* . . . . That the trial of your faith might be found unto praise and honour and glory at the appearing of Jesus Christ:

> Whom having *not* seen ye love; to whom, though now ye see him *not*, yet believing, ye rejoice with joy unspeakable and full of glory.

Full of glory - that is the meaning of ascensiontide. We do not know the glory which is to be revealed. We only know it concerns those things (in Peter's words) that 'the angels desire to look into'. We cannot guess what transformations these are. But when we make the sign of anticipation, we have a foretaste of the heavenly banquet and of a heaven and earth which are full of the glory of God.

Whit-Sunday (Pentecost): 1.
Inspiriting

'... O my people, I will open your graves ... and shall put my spirit in
you, and ye shall live ...'
Ezekiel 37:12 and 14

A while ago, in a diocesan theological group we were discussing
what we are concerned with when we preach from the words of
scripture. What are we up to? I suggested that we were searching
through scripture to look for the fundamental forms of hope and
frustration, aligning ourselves with hope. It seems to me that St.
Paul is concerned with precisely that. The great contrasts he
deploys are death and life, bondage and liberty, suffering and
glory. We are, he says, in travail between death, suffering and
bondage - and life, liberty and glory. And theology itself divides
into two great sectors, the theology of the cross and the theology
of glory. It takes for its thematic material frustration and hope; and
it chooses hope. The church's year also turns on a contrast between
frustration and hope. The forty days of Lent and the Passion are
focused on privation, trial, suffering and death. The fifty days of
Easter which conclude at Pentecost focus on life and resurrection,
exaltation and the freedom of the spirit. They are like double
facing panels around the cross on the altar, picturing the two sides
of faith.

In the same way, the whole biblical story alternates between
frustration and hope. At the beginning and the end are vistas and
visions of perfection, embodied in the harmonious garden and the
heavenly city. But from the end of the beginning to the beginning
of the end there is a pattern of loss and recovery. There is, first of
all, the massive contrast which dominates the whole pattern: 'As
in Adam all die even so in Christ shall all be made alive'. Within
that alternation between first representative man and second
representative man runs the persistent pattern of frustration and
hope, exile and return, bondage and liberty, privation and plenitude, bruising and glory. *Here* is the dead valley of the dry bones;

74

there the wind blows and we have the exceeding great army of the living God.

Israel lies in the bondage of Egypt. Then it crosses the Red Sea. Israel wanders in the wilderness. Then it enters the Promised Land. Israel is in exile. Then it returns to build up the waste places of Jerusalem. That is all the history of the first man, constantly trying to find the way out of bondage and out of the corruption of the body and the soul. And then we have the history of the second man, dramatized around the contrast of Lent and Easter. He, too, was in the wilderness. He, too, entered into glory. It behoved Christ to suffer; it behoved Christ to enter into glory. This corruptible put on incorruption: 'For as in Adam all die, even so in Christ shall all be made alive'.

It was Paul who directed us to the crux of this extraordinary history. We are, he says, in travail between frustration and hope. We groan between the bruising and the glory. And that cross of frustration *is* the hope of glory. There is no God up there in glory while we are terribly bruised. There is a God who is terribly bruised, whose cross is His glory. I glory, says Paul, only in the cross of Christ. It is here, if anywhere, that God must be and is made manifest. If He cannot be manifest in the blood and the suffering at the centre of the human predicament then we only have an almighty overseer, not a loving and redeeming God.

So, as we stand here looking at the completed second panel of hope, facing the first panel of frustration, we have to remember the hinge on which it turns, and the crux on which it hangs. There is no happy, easy celebration of the glorious ascension of Christ and the free outpouring of the spirit, without a knowledge of the centrality of the cross. We are not in some happy, healthy, holy condition, on the other side of frustration. *God knows* we are not. In Paul's words we groan and we travail. But we are, nevertheless, creatures of promise. We have chosen hope and been seized by hope. So we, in our own lives repeat this alternation, visible throughout history, between the reality of bruising and the hope of glory. As we suffer with Christ, says Paul, so we may also be glorified with Him.

The whole of the panel that reaches from Easter to Pentecost (and beyond to now) pictures us as creatures of promise and children of hope. It says that these bones can live. Most of us feel like Ezekiel, that the valley is full of bones and that they are very dry. The word that comes to us, as to him, has to do with being breathed into. The signs are those of wind and fire. The vocabulary of the season is composed of inspiration, creativity, wisdom, freedom, filling and outpouring. The master image is of a world unified by a common language. Turn your face from the babel of confusion and fragmentation to the common spirit and the shared language which spreads abroad from God's Jerusalem to all the nations on earth. All of us are 'in Adam' dead, frustrated, beaten, and very dry. But as 'in Adam all die, even so in Christ shall all be made *alive*'. The in-filling and out-pouring of the spirit is just this being 'made alive'. O my people, says Ezekiel, I will 'open your graves . . . and shall put my spirit in you and ye shall live'.

That alternation of death and life, dryness and inspiration, frustration and hope, bruising and glory, lies at the heart of the Eucharist. It contains the facing panels of privation and plenitude, turning and hinging on the glory of the cross. The Eucharist offers a foretaste of the heavenly banquet in which all sit down to the Kingdom of God and share a common speech. In that banquet we invoke the entry of the spirit of wind and of fire to inform and to transform the feast with the presence of God. Each fragment of broken bread we absorb is a little colony of divinity placed in a divided, bruised and fragmented world. It is marked with a cross, we sign it with a cross. It signifies a world redeemed, unified, and restored, remade in the image and likeness of its Creator and of its Redeemer.

Whit-Sunday (Pentecost): 2.
New Generations

'And Joshua . . . was full of the spirit of wisdom; for Moses had
laid his hands on him . . .'
Deuteronomy 34:9

'. . . I go my way . . . [but] when he, the Spirit of truth is come, he
will guide you into all truth . . .'
St. John 16:5 and 13

These texts are both concerned with a parting of the ways and the assurance of continuity. In the one, Moses is at the end of his mission and passes on his task to Joshua by a *laying on of hands.* In the other, Jesus envisages the end of his physical presence with the disciples and promises a new *guidance in the spirit.* The founders of Judaism and of Christianity come to the point of transition and they have to make sure their work continues. In the one case, the vehicle of continuity is the particular people of Israel; in the other case it is the universal people of God. We do not know, of course, how much Moses or Jesus foresaw of what was ahead. They had a vision, not a blueprint or a history book of the future. Moses had a gleaming sight of a land of promise from Mt. Pisgah, into which he could never enter. Jesus had faith in the seed he had sown, which would grow into the tree for the healing of all nations.

So that is a common element in the two stories: a new phase, a transition, a passing on. And we immediately recognize the two ways in which that passing on is effected: one by the laying on of hands, the other by the transmission of the spirit. The Christian Church has usually appealed to both the continuity of the laying on of hands and to the sense of being joined in one and the same spirit. It respects the formal handing on by the placing of hands on the head of those who carry the truth forward; and it recognizes a spiritual band of brothers whose spark leaps from head to head and heart to heart.

The trouble is that these two great principles of continuity can be in conflict: the charismatic and spontaneous invocation of the spirit can war against the traditional chain of authority handed down, literally, from generation to generation. Those who feel they are visited by the spirit can ignore the deep wisdom embedded in the traditional institutions and the forms by which that wisdom is handed on. Those who handle the reins of traditional authority can rule too tightly and forget the freedom of the spirit and even ignore the spirit of truth.

Ideally the formal act and the spiritual transmission complement each other. Historically, however, these have been periods of deadening formalism, in which holy things are handed on mechanically, followed by periods of enthusiastic fracture, in which a babel of voices bursts out, breaking the holy vessels, sundering the Church, and losing the accumulated richness of inherited form and ancient wisdom. And the contrast is more complicated than that. Often the inherited forms are far from mechanical or dead; they are containers of profound spiritual energies, quietly and continuously fertilizing the soul. They allow space for meditation; there is a largeness about them in which the spirit may walk in ordered freedom. And often, by contrast, the enthusiastic partisans of the untrammelled spirit end up in closed circles of their own, reliant on their own temporary resources, and gradually turning their happy fraternities into authoritarian tyrannies. They denigrate the long line of settled authority vested in fathers-in-God; they elevate their own circles forgetting they can be inturned and lead nowhere. Of course, the rule of the fathers has often been dreadful. But the camaraderie of the brothers has often been worse, because one brother generally turns out to be so much bigger than all the rest.

Theologically, and sociologically - you can think in terms of the circle and the line: both necessary, both dangerous. The *circle* is the principle of human fraternity in which we all face each other; the *line* breaks through the circle, like the sweep of a church from west to east, orienting all equally towards the one transcendent source of light, taking the eye to what is above and beyond mortal sight. And the two can come together. The other evening, I saw black Pentecostals filling Southwark Cathedral with the effervescence of the spirit, but that marvellous concerted symphony of praise was based on the sense of form and order in all present, *and* on the long vista that took the eye, dramatically, from west to east, guiding it to the common source of order and joy. On the one hand the service said: rejoice in the spirit; on the other, it said 'People, look east'.

So we have these twin principles, call them if you like, spirit and form, circle and line. And like all the great complementary truths they are open to the gravest misuse and to perverse one-sidedness. I do not know if you are like me, but whenever I hear a formalist claim that there is only one institutional succession equipped with a rule book of infallible truth, I feel stirred up with a sense of spiritual independence and reasoned enquiry. And, equally, whenever I hear some group of people claiming to dispense the latest revelations of the Holy Spirit, I want to test their claims against the long run of accumulated tradition and rationality.

How do we avoid one-sidedness? First we appeal to order and continuity: the laying on of hands, what is handed on, handed down - in short, tradition. It is the principle of memory and recitation. Do this in *memory*; recollect the great events. For the old Israel recall and re-enact the events of the Passover, the exodus, and the entry to a Promised Land; for the new Israel: recall and re-enact the supper of the Lord, the passage through death, the signs of His coming Kingdom. These are the great charters, the Magna Cartas, to be displayed, remembered, re-enacted. They are the unnegotiable bases of hope, without which the spirit will lose its way and die in the wilderness, chasing phantoms. They are the deposit, the treasure to be *handed on*, from generation to generation, so that the New Testament itself must begin by placing its newness *in line*. Why else should Matthew chapter 1, verse 1 say: 'The book of the generation of Jesus Christ, the son of David, the son of Abraham', and why else should the epistle to the Hebrews say 'by faith Abel, by faith Abraham, by faith Moses . . .'?

And yet at the heart of tradition itself is inserted the Holy Spirit of truth. As Moses laid his hand on Joshua he passed on a spirit of wisdom. As Jesus spoke of parting from His disciples he invoked the spirit which would lead men into all truth. For neither Moses nor Jesus was the task finished or the truth complete. The one stood on the borders of promise, overlooking an unknown land; the other stood on the edge of a universal kingdom. Wisdom, reason and the spirit of truth find yet more to break from the Word. They reflect on the deposit of faith, they interpret the great charter. They seek the intersection of the eternal and temporal, finding its relevance in new circumstances. They test ancient truths against new knowledge, and passing trends against accumulated wisdom. Truth *remains* but is never complete; we do not *have* all truth; we are promised to be led *into* it.

All that was *necessary* had been done - by Moses and by Jesus. Mission accomplished. 'It is finished.' But that end was, and is, just the beginning. 'I go my way . . . but the Spirit, He will guide you into all truth.'

Whit-Sunday (Pentecost): 3.
Dove Talk

'And the Spirit of God moved upon the face of the waters.'
Genesis 1 : 2

'And they were all filled with the Holy Ghost, and began to speak with
other tongues, as the Spirit gave them utterance.'
Acts 2:4

'The Spirit itself bears witness with our spirit, that we are the
children of God.'
Romans 8:16

Whit-Sunday is the birthday of the universal Church. Just as the
law which was given on Sinai constituted Israel a chosen nation,
so the Spirit which was given at Pentecost constituted the disciples
a universal Church. The sign of that universal scope was an
outburst of energy breaking down all the confusions of language
and culture. Every human being of whatever kind or colour
standing there in Jerusalem that day was able to pick up a new
language of promise. Pentecost was an annunciation, an announcement, addressed to every creature.

So my Pentecostal theme has to be the breaking down of all
the barriers to communication. Pentecost was *nuclear* in that it
unlocked latent powers and opened up a new era. It was the
flashpoint, not of threat as at Los Alamos in 1944, but of spiritual
promise. The fundamental terms of the promise were quite
unequivocal: love and life, hope and joy, wisdom and power,
patience and peace. So its sign, its logo (or logos if you like), had
to be the dove. Christianity was launched under the logo of a shy
white bird whose presence promises peace.

But how do we ourselves tap in to this outburst of energy and
pick up the manifestations of the Spirit? How do we recognize and
share in creativity and in redemptive action? Here I want to say
that the Spirit can be known and shared not only when named and

identified in the Church but when he acts anonymously in our everyday experience. This means, first of all, that the dove descends when we assemble around the holy table to take in our immortal food. But the dove also descends whenever we encounter beauty, creativity, or integrity. The bird is in flight at all times and in all places, accompanied by clear markers in holy houses, and accompanied elsewhere simply by our sense of a presence, or of an opening, or of something extended in a gesture of care. So you can see the dove beautifully arrayed in the ecclesiastical enclosure, and equally see him moving abroad in the open air. It is for us to learn how to recognize his presence and his passage, saying to ourselves: 'There goes the dove, the peacebringer.'

I want, therefore, to give just two examples: one of the dove appearing when invoked and called upon in the community of the faithful, and another of a flight carried out beyond the usual boundaries of faith. The first example is from a television programme from a church for the deaf in Falkirk. To appreciate the power of this extraordinary communication you have to imagine the unbroken and total silence of the world of the deaf, without the familiar tones of the human voice, without the sounds which identify a cracking twig or a breaking wave, without bird song or music. As I write this all the channels of my sense are open and receptive. But close down the sound channel and I would be shut up in my skull. Part of me would have gone dead.

And yet for the deaf people in Falkirk, who had undergone so drastic a restriction, the world had become meaningful and vibrant through gesture. They had mastered communication like a conductor masters a score and then conveys his message by rhythmic movements, by the precise sweep of the hands, the admonitions and coaxings of the fingers. The deaf spoke with their hands and eyes, and even took part in hymns through rhythm. For anyone watching this extraordinary performance it was a miracle in which the tongue of the dumb sang. Over it all was written, without shadow of doubt, the logo of the holy spirit. Through the power of creativity limitation had been converted into opportunity, and confinement turned into freedom.

My other example is taken from outside any community of faith and from quite the other end of the spectrum of communication. Just recently a master class for young singers was held at Aldeburgh in Suffolk, tutored by the pianist Murray Perahia. In that tiny town young people had gathered from every corner of the earth: Koreans and Japanese, Americans and English, all of them joined by just one thing: the universal language of music. Their hearts and minds were filled with an eloquence beyond all the specific information conveyed in ordinary speech. Murray Perahia was rehearsing the singers in Mozart's 'Così fan tutte' and he began by trying to indicate the dynamics he wanted through normal talk. But there came a moment when words failed him and all he could do was to sit down at the piano. What he then created was one miracle after another of perfect shaping. Every movement of his mind was realized in unfettered expression. The poise and the mastery, the perfectly judged tensions and releases, conveyed total freedom. And yet once the phrases were completed it seemed as if no alternative had ever been possible. Just now I used the word 'dynamics', and that is simply the Greek word for 'spirit', the same word used to describe that extraordinary outburst of energy and communication two thousand years ago.

Every moment we feel the breath of life in the gestures of the deaf or the creativity of the gifted, or in any act whatever of care or offering or blessing, we are in correspondence with the universal Spirit. We, literally, co-respond. All of us are touched by tongues of fire and know the descent of the dove. For 'the Spirit itself bears witness with our spirit that we are the children of God'.

Trinity: 1.
The Presence

'Holy, holy, holy, Lord God Almighty, which was, and is,
and is to come.'
Revelation 4 : 8

Consider what we pass through in the great sector of the Church's year which runs from the Advent to Pentecost. We go on a journey which began with the coming of the promised Christ and was consummated in the coming of the promised spirit. It commenced in the gift of a child and concluded in the spiritual gift of unity, love, wisdom, power, and peace. That journey had a turning point which was *also* a gift: the offering of Christ's body to humankind on His cross. That is the turning point of the whole movement from the offer of a baby to the offer of a spirit. The cross is the great hinge on which hangs all else. It is the fracture of God's image in humankind. The centre of it all is a moment of breaking and therefore of giving.

The other day I was asked what the movements of bodies and hands meant at different points in the Eucharist: genuflections, bowings, signs of the cross and the elevation. Think of them in terms of this journey from the gift of a baby to the gift of a spirit. Suppose there are three movements in the symphony of the Church's year. There is first the coming of Christ: his Advent. There is then the testing of Christ, his privation, isolation, and death, which we call Lent. There is then the upraising of Christ and His glorification, which we call Easter. So we have a sequence of gifts: the baby, the wounded man, the exalted man and his universal spirit. In that sequence you have moved from the very small, embodied in the tiny child to that which fills and fulfils the whole universe.

Think of those three movements of Advent, Lent and Easter and then think of the movements in which we engage in the Eucharist. I know that some of us make these movements in the heart, some with their bodies. But the density of symbolism, for body and for heart, clusters at the point of God's entry into human life, *and was incarnate*; at the point where the image of God is fractured, *this is my body which is given*; and at the point where the divine in man is upraised and elevated in glory. And it is at the moment of fracture that we make a complete obeisance. Here priests and people kneel together to say: *here* is the crux.

So now we have the picture; the three-fold movement of the year, which is also a three-fold movement of this drama we call the Eucharist: entry, bruising, exaltation - from the smallest to that which fills and unites the whole universe. How very small this little fragment is; how tiny this body. Break it and it fills and feeds the world.

Pentecost is almost, *almost*, the conclusion of the last movement, the end of the fifty days of Easter. It is the feast of infilling and outpouring. The tiny, confined spark blazes into the world-consuming fire. The flame of universal love breaks *out*; and it breaks *down* all the barriers and separations of language and human speech. Of course it is the same creative spirit that brooded on the waters and brought order out of chaos; the same holy spirit that entered into the generation of Christ; the same spirit of love which upheld the wounded man on his cross; the same spirit of life which upraised and exalted him. Throughout the whole movement of time, the movement of the Church's year, and our own movement this morning, there is this one spirit of creativity, holiness, love, and life eternal and undefeatable.

But there is one further element, and one beyond which we cannot go. It is the presence of God. It crowns time and the Church's year and the movement of our liturgy. With the gifts of creation, and the grace of God in Christ, comes the presence. We make another complete act of obeisance with the sense that we are, all of us, overshadowed with the power of the Most High. These gifts of bread and wine, which are the fruits of nature and which are also the body of Christ, become for us the presence of God in His temple. The elements are charged with all the fullness of God. The little company of earth is united with the whole

company of heaven. When we eat of the food of angels we hear the
song of the angels.

    Therefore with angels and archangels,
    And with all the company of heaven,
    we laud and magnify thy glorious name
    evermore, praising thee and saying:
      Holy, holy, holy, Lord God of Hosts,
      Heaven and earth are full of thy glory.
      Glory be to thee, o Lord most high.

Trinity: 2.
The Opening Door

*'I looked, and, behold, a door was opened in heaven and . . . I heard
. . . as it were . . . a trumpet talking with me.'*
Revelation 4:1

The Christian year is a dramatic cycle. From Advent until Trinity
we have passed through all the phases of the cycle. In Advent the
year begins in marvellous anticipations fulfilled in the birth of the
Holy Child; it continues in testing and in suffering; it reaches a
glorious final act in resurrection, ascension and exaltation. Each
phase evokes a *picture* in our mind: the watchman with his
midnight cry, shepherds and wise men on their journeys, a lonely
figure tested by phantoms and fantasies in the wilderness, the
outstretched arms of the Saviour, the resurrected Christ present in
the garden early in the morning and again walking beside His
disciples in the evening.

Each phase, then, has its picture: an icon to focus and anchor
our imagination. All we have to do is to listen to a story and watch
as the pictures are turned over from beginning to end. Christianity
is the tale of the loving purposes of God, with *illustrations*. Or, if
you prefer, it is a miracle play, with tableaux at each crisis in the
action.

On the feast of the Trinity the story is complete and we write
the Amen at the foot of the last page. The Son is reunited in the
bosom of the Father, manhood is taken up into Godhead, and the
manifold energies of the spirit are spread abroad in mankind and
all creation. The flame of sacred love is kindled in the hearts of all
believers. But somehow the conclusion is difficult. We are now
present in the spirit before the First, the Last and the Living One,
but we lack an image. We have passed beyond pictures into the
realm of the luminous sign: the three-in-oneness of the blessed
Trinity. It is the sign, the formula, the ascription which begins the

Christian sermon, which concludes our singing of psalms and making of prayers.

What then is the role of this luminous sign, in the name of which we preach and pray? Well, it is a summary of all that has gone before. In the physical world the energy mass equation, $E = mc^2$, summarizes and unifies a vast range of experience and testing; so, too, in the world of the spirit, the sign of the mysterious three-in-one summarizes and unifies a vast range of experience and testing. It brings together everything thus far. So, those first anticipations of a birth, the testings in the wilderness and on the cross, the release of the energies of the spirit, together with our response to and our reliance upon the patterns of the world of nature, all these are pervaded by the oneness of God. Whether we look over the vast panorama of the visible creation or the intimate theatre of our redemption, there is, over all, through all and in all, one God, blessed for ever. I could compose a litany to express this:

The Spirit that moved on the face of the waters: He also is God.
The inspiration of the holy prophets: He also is God.
The holy and vulnerable child Jesus: He also is God.
The man wounded for our transgressions: He also is God.
The Spirit of wisdom, holiness and love: He also is God.

Trinity is the feast of that many which is also one: '*Over* all, *through* all and *in* all'. To those great prepositions 'over', 'through', and 'in' we add 'first', and 'last': today is the feast of the First and the Last and the Living One.

I hope it is now clear why we cannot have an illustration for Trinity. We cannot possibly picture or image what is present in every picture, or tell a story about something which underlies every turn in the narrative. We can only affirm that in this picture and that story we recognize the same sign, the sole signature, the common unifying mark, the one God.

What more might we say about this luminous sign which unites our experience of stone and star, our moral being, and the spiritual transformation wrought by God in Christ? We can use only one word to characterize it: 'holy'. As 'glory' is the word which belongs to ascension, so 'holy' is the word which belongs to the Triune God.

That word 'holy' is a *transformer*. Just as mankind in Christ can be taken into God so the whole of our experience can be made holy. It is capable of *trans*-formation by the presence. In so much of our experience - in the city, the home, the meal - we are conscious only of the great absence. But in truth, there lies in that experience of city, home, and meal a real presence. The most holy God enters into our experience to effect an alteration.

But *what* alteration? Let me illustrate from William Blake. Blake said of some people that when they saw the sun they saw only something shaped rather like a golden guinea. But I, he said, see ten thousand times ten thousand crying 'Holy, Holy, Holy is the Lord of Hosts'. One day, William Blake was in the city watching charity children entering into St. Pauls, and he wrote:

O what a multitude they seemed,
These flowers of London Town
Seated in companies they sit
With radiance all their own.
The hum of multitudes was there,
But multitudes of lambs
Thousands of little boys and girls
Raising their innocent hands
Now like a mighty wind they raise
To heaven the voice of song,
Or like harmonious thunderings
The seats of heaven among.

Blake found the holy city, New Jerusalem, coming down in London. Here we have all the pictures of heaven in the Book of Revelation, trans-forming our experience into knowledge of holiness: the great multitude which no man can number, the radiance, the raising of hands, the mighty wind of the spirit, lightnings and thunderings, the great song which sweeps across the seats of heaven.

In our ordinary life the angelic hymn of the *Sanctus* is shut off behind closed doors. We are deaf to the blessing, to the honour, the glory and the power. But if we look and listen a door begins to open in heaven and we discover the pleasure of creation:

I looked . . . and behold, a door was opened in heaven and I
heard . . . as it were, a trumpet talking with me.

PART II
THE CHRISTIAN EXPERIENCE

Grace: 1.
The Open Invitation

'. . . Believe on the Lord Jesus Christ, and thou shalt be saved . . .'
Acts 16 : 31

This is one of the great sentences of evangelical religion. I put it that way because we all of us have our own Bible, which we have quarried from the original text to support a particular understanding of Christianity. When I was brought up in an evangelical home, I was convinced I knew the Bible. In fact, what I knew were the texts which were the foundations of the evangelical revival. Some of the many Bibles in our house had those texts underlined in red. This particular text was almost certainly in red letters. It belongs to that select group you may expect to find on stations, almost as frequently as John 3 : 16: 'God so loved the world that he gave his only-begotten son that whosoever liveth and believeth in him should not perish but have everlasting life'. Indeed, it is almost the same text: life and salvation come by Christ, who is the gift of God, and by faith in Him.

You may have noticed that I have already altered one word. I have changed 'belief' in Christ to *'faith'* in Christ. And that perhaps is what somebody who brings an evangelical background to his understanding of the Bible might be expected to do. 'Belief' in the evangelical reading of the Bible is almost the same as 'faith'. To believe is to have faith. Looking at the readings for today, I turned by accident to the lectionary of the Prayer Book, and that would have offered me the key text of the Reformation. It was the fifth chapter of St. Paul to the Romans, which is his great exposition of justification by faith, beginning 'Being justified by faith we have peace with God through our Lord Jesus Christ'. All these texts, Acts 16 : 31, John 3 : 16, Romans 5 are about salvation, about life and peace through Christ. There are the thunderous synonyms of the Reformation: life, peace, salvation, justification, and all 'in Christo', in Christ. This is the explosive mandate of the gospel: you are saved, you are justified by faith alone and grace alone: *sola fide, sola gratia.* To 'faith' we add yet another great word 'grace', not quite a synonym, but it belongs in this marvellous cluster: faith, salvation, justification, grace - and all of them the foundation of life, peace and immortality. Here is the core of the promise.

But what does it mean? And with what is it contrasted? Take the *contrasts* first. Faith is contrasted with *belief,* and with *works.* But how can it be contrasted with 'belief'? 'Belief', after all, is part of our text: 'Believe in the Lord Jesus Christ and thou shalt be saved'. It depends on what you mean by 'belief'. 'Belief' may mean assent to a proposition: when you believe something you suppose such and such to be the case. You have some kind of scientific or historical or everyday knowledge. 'Belief' as we have it in our text does not refer to knowledge. It means 'faith', which is why I brought in the parallel texts to show that we are saved by faith, not by beliefs. There is an important place for correct beliefs, but it is not this most central place occupied by faith. Faith is the fundamental act of *trust.* It is a movement of the soul, not the reasoned consent of the mind. It is what is covered by that other great evangelical word 'conversion'. What does 'conversion' mean? It is the act of turning to God, through Christ and in Christ, in a moment of total *trust.* In the end, faced with the creeds and the propositions, we have to say 'I do not *know,* but I do *trust'.* St. Paul could *not* say that by beliefs or by belief you are saved. When we have the word 'belief' it must mean you are to turn and to trust. That then is the first great contrast. Belief as an assent of the mind is below faith, that is, faith understood as an act of the whole person, made in trust and in hope.

The second contrast is with 'works', meaning obedience to the law and virtuous action. Of course, there is a place for virtue and for obedience to the law just as there is a place for right belief. But here we are dealing with the language of Christian priorities. Faith is *prior.* At the root of Christianity is this act of faith, which is the stirring of godliness within you. It is less an act, than the emergence within you of a pure gift. 'By grace are ye saved through faith, and that not of yourselves; it is the gift of God which worketh in you.' There is another red-letter text if you like: another foundation of the gospel. Of course, evangelicalism has turned these promises of salvation into stereotyped repetitions and thoughtless cliches. But, nevertheless, they break through all these emotional reiterations as the crux, the kernel, the foundation stone. *There is no other foundation given.*

Faith, then, is prior to belief and prior to works: faith is the emergence of your response to the gift of God in Christ, and that emergence is itself a gift. At that moment, when it stirs in you and you throw away every support except this trust, you have the grace of God working in you. And when the gospel speaks of faith in Christ it means that the knowledge of God as gift and as grace has come to you in Him. He is the great lover of all mankind, who emptied Himself of all but love and gave His life that all might live in Him; He comes alive in you as pure gift. The Christ in you comes alive as you know Him to be God's first and final word. You are covered; you are accepted; all righteousness is yours. And here, of course, we come to yet another evangelical promise, with perhaps rather a forbidding sound: imputed righteousness.

But however forbidding it may sound, the meaning is not forbidding. It is accepting. You are accepted. And it has absolutely nothing to do with anything you have done, or can do. You come before God with nothing. If for one moment you start to thrust forward some virtuous deed, some ritual performance, some obedience to the law, you have lost hold on His absolute mercy and His grace. Nothing else is required than faith alone and grace alone, as made real for you in the saving Word pronounced in Christ. You may, like the jailer, be in prison, but this Word sets you free. 'Believe in the Lord Jesus Christ and thou shalt be saved.'

Grace: 2.
Being Accepted

'... joy shall be in heaven over one sinner that repenteth, more than over ninety and nine just persons ...'
St. Luke 15:7

I want to respond in a simple and direct way to this gospel. One of the startling things about the gospel is its *unfairness*. Provided you have been a sinner and then repent, heaven will be merry and joyful over you. Go away from home and live like a pig, you only have to come back and your heavenly father will throw a party. Laze around for years and turn up to work for the final stint and you will have the same reward as those who have slaved away all their natural lives. Just sit around deeply absorbed in fascinating talk instead of getting the house straight and you will be highly commended.

But, now, go round the other way and see what happens. Just see what happens if you obey the law from your youth up. You have performed up to specification: yet what do you get? You will be told you should sell up everything you have and join the first century equivalent of a peace convoy. Pay your dues, obey the conventions, keep the rules, live by the book, carry out all the obligations of a good and decent citizen, and you will find you do not have a ticket for the great feast. It seems that instead of good citizens, sitting like excellent guildsmen at a city banquet, the feast will be thrown open to a bunch of scruffs brought in off the highway. Worse than that, if you claim this just is not fair, you will be asked who you are to start complaining.

But this is the gospel nevertheless. Let us put it another way, and not in terms of what is and is not fair. Let us put it in terms of living by the book, and striking a bargain. What the gospel proclaims is: live by the book and you will have the book thrown at you, and a lot more. Strike a bargain in which you put your virtues onto the scales, and the scales will turn against you.

It could all be summed up in the case of Judas, the book-keeper, versus the woman who anointed Christ. Judas has the best possible argument. He does, indeed, live by the book: he actually is the accountant for this disreputable peace convoy. And then this woman, whoever she was, breaks all the rules with a sudden impulse of grace: she pours precious ointment all over her precious Lord. At that moment, Judas becomes the spokesman of all careful virtue. *This is sheer waste.* Think of what good this precious stuff could do if it were made over to the deprived and the impoverished. Remember the inner city! And at that moment, challenged by virtue, by the book, by good citizenship, Christ spoke the gospel. Whatever else this woman has done, this act of hers *is not waste.* It is the fulfilment of everything she is: it is pure grace. So, to Judas, measure for measure; so, to the woman, grace for grace.

The Church cannot fully absorb this. Always the Church has a hankering after measure for measure and a terror of grace for grace. Of course, it will go on telling these stories of the clash between measure and grace, but it dare go no further. When Christ responded to that act of daring and wasteful love, he went on to say, with equal daring, that wherever the gospel was proclaimed this moment would be remembered. A Church with sufficient courage and moral imagination would have made this one of the sacraments. We might have had four great sacraments: there could have been the gift of Christ's body in the great feast, and the passage from death to life in the waters of baptism, and there could also have been the washing of the feet and the pouring of the ointment. The commands were there: wash each other's feet and remember the pouring of the ointment wherever the gospel is preached in the whole world. But this gospel is just too much of a good thing. The terror of sovereign grace is too great.

And just as the Church cannot absorb this, neither can we. We come to take the gift of Christ full of measure for measure and with book-keeping in our hearts. Either we feel we have no right here because we are condemned by the book, or perhaps we even think we have measured up to the measure of Christ. In either case, we have no sense - either of how far we are from God or of how close

He is to us. We let the law fill us either with apprehension or with pride. We can draw back out of our fear of the law or come forward in the pride of having measured up. Yet, all we are asked to do is to give and receive. Grace is all sufficient, and nothing but grace is sufficient. That is the only path to the joy of heaven: 'sufficient, sovereign, saving, grace'.

This is not an attack on rate-paying or on lawfulness or on virtue. It is not an invitation to join the activities of the hippies around Stonehenge, supposing - as seems unlikely - you had a mind to that sort of thing. Personally, I prefer dealing with virtuous people who keep their promises rather than with rogues who do not. But the gospel forbids us to approach God clutching to the law book, thinking either of what we have done or haven't done. It proclaims rather that we are very far off from grace and that grace is already there, offered to us without bargain, without conditions, and without price. It is like the pouring out of ointment: priceless. Beyond the world of the market where everything is measure for measure there is the world of grace for grace. And the gift is there for the taking, provided we are neither too proud nor too afraid. That is *all*: neither pride nor fear, but confidence and acceptance. As you join the feast, you join the community of those who are under grace and not under the law. You are acceptable and you are accepted. If you can bear it, *nothing* stands between you and the love of God. 'Take, eat, this is my body which is given for you.'

Nature.
Manifold Works

'O Lord, how manifold are thy works! in wisdom hast thou
made them all . . .'
Psalm 104:24

I want to consider the manifold works of God, especially as they are manifest in creation. The world as we know it has been *ordained*, which is to say that it has been placed in an order, *disposed* after a certain manner. It comes, in the words of Milton, from the 'unsearchable dispose of highest wisdom'. The psalmists had precisely this sense of *ordination*: 'When I consider the moon and the stars which thou hast *ordained* what is man that thou art mindful of him?' For them the all-wise and all-mighty source of everything that *is* had hurled the world into an amazing order. It was their pleasure lovingly to enumerate the works of God in their variety and their goodness. *Benedicite omnia opera*: 'O all ye Works of the Lord, bless ye the Lord'. Like Adam naming the animals one by one they looked on the goodness of each divine work - green things, wells, seas and floods, whales, fowls of the air - and saw that each one 'blessed the Lord'.

There are two great hymns of creation in the Old Testament. One is by the writer of the Book of Job and the other by the writer of Psalm 104. In the Book of Job the writer celebrates the superabundant bounty of creation, recognizing that this arena of divine power is vast and mysterious beyond anything we can imagine. Man stands before it over-awed at the amazing economy of the divine creativity from the fine detail of the 'goodly wings' of the peacock to astronomical immensity: the sweet influences of the Pleiades and the bands of Orion. In Psalm 104, the pleasure of the psalmist is found more perhaps in a sense of landscape and the different orders of creation that inhabit it, each after their own kind. Asses quench their thirst at springs, the wild goats take refuge in the high hills, the beasts of the forest 'creep forth in the night', and man, the last work of God, gladdens his heart with wine, anoints his body with oil and 'goeth forth unto his work' and to his labour until evening.

And all this is a celebration of everything that the Lord of the year and the Lord of the tides has *ordained*: it is an awed response to order, and to all that we may survey but cannot grasp in its infinite greatness. Of course, we know that we do not only respond to creation in its obvious beneficence. There is also a fecund and death-dealing savagery in the economy of nature:

Pike, three inches long, perfect
Pike in all parts green tigering the gold.
Killers from the egg: the malevolent aged grin.
They dance on the surface among the flies.

Modern man has developed the doctrine of creation, enriching his sense of divinity and extending the arena of God's work. Out of the Old Testament view of God's initial and powerful ordination of everything that is, has come a new sense of communion with the manifold works of God. Humankind has discovered visible traces of the invisible God, which speak not only of ordination but of harmony, unity and reverence. For centuries from Augustine to Petrarch this faculty of apprehending God in His world lay dormant. Nearly seven centuries ago, it was unheard of for a man to climb a mountain for its own sake. Then Petrarch with three companions did so, ascending Mt Ventoux, near Avignon. And, it was, says Jacob Burckhardt, as if 'a veil had been lifted from nature'. There he had what we today would call a 'peak experience'. For us since Petrarch, mountains and seas have become confessionals and sacraments of communion with the world.

Part of that experience of nature which we first recovered nearly seven centuries ago has been a re-entry into paradise. The myth of Adam in paradise tells us that traces of an ancient union of humankind and nature lie all around us. For a moment, we are relieved of our sense of corruption and disharmony to enter the world as it first issued from the hand of the Creator. There is something early, innocent and angelic about this experience, as though we had taken our first look on the first morning. 'Morning has broken, like the first morning.' Henry Vaughan speaks of it in a poem which says we must rise early to know the world as it was in God's original paradise:

Walk with thy fellow-creatures: note the *hush*
And *whispers* amongst them. There's not a *spring*,
Or *leaf* but hath his *morning-hymn*; each *bush*
And *oak* knows I AM; canst thou not sing?

For Henry Vaughan the world hymns the Creator. The world is quick with life.

Birds, beasts, all things
Adore him in their kinds.
Thus all is hurled
In sacred *hymns* and *order*, the great *chime*
And *symphony* of nature.

'Chime' and 'symphony': the two words mean 'sounding together'. This experience of God is one in which all the disparate jarring sounds are joined in harmony.

Wordsworth, who opened up a whole universe of response to our world, called this sense of nature a *ministry*. The world as it is *ordained* by God offered him - and us - a *ministry*. As he perused the Book of Nature, he read there a 'higher language'. 'Let me dare speak a higher language . . .'. He wrote:

I looked for universal things; perused
The common countenance of earth and sky
Earth, nowhere unembellished by some trace
Of that first Paradise whence man was driven . . .

This 'ministry' comes not only in 'our angel-infancy' but also returns as a restoration for those who are mature and have experienced corruption. Returning from a pass in Scotland he writes:

There's not a nook within this solemn Pass
But were an apt *confessional* for One
Taught by his summer spent, his autumn gone
That Life is but a tale of morning grass
Withered at eve.

He writes also of the hushed evening when:

The holy time is quiet as a Nun
Breathless with adoration;

There is, he believed, 'a *presence* that disturbs us with the joy of elevated thoughts . . .'.

Here we see all those words which an earlier generation would have thought proper only to the sacramental worship of God - ministry, solemnity, reverence, and confessional, holiness, adoration, presence - re-used to express joy in creation. And here, of course, there is a danger: that the mind may rest in nature, not in nature's God; that it may forget in the gracefulness of created things the grace of God in our redemption. There is a beauty which is not mortal beauty; the beatific vision of God's infinite grace in Christ. There are the marks and traces of a divine love, which 'moves the sun and all the stars'. Gerard Manley Hopkins says that behind mortal beauty there is always 'God's better beauty, grace'.

So, there are two *Benedicite's* in the Christian religion. One belongs to the realm of physical *necessity* and the miracle of nature:

> O all ye works of the Lord, *bless* ye the Lord. Praise him and magnify him for ever.

The other belongs to the realm of human freedom and the miracle of divine grace.

> *Blessed* be the God and Father of our Lord Jesus Christ, which according to his abundant mercy hath begotten us again, unto a lively hope by the resurrection of Jesus Christ from the dead, to an inheritance incorruptible and undefiled, that fadeth not away, reserved in heaven for you.

Conversion.
Turning Round

'They that sow in tears shall reap in joy.'
Psalm 126:5

I want to think about conversion. The ideas we have about conversion come, above all, from St. Paul's sudden illumination on the way to Damascus; and the redemptive language we use is above all his. It is a language which can make us uneasy and even afraid. We are afraid because conversion and the preaching of redemption conjure up pictures of fanatical enthusiasts manipulating crowds into paroxysms of emotion; and also because we have a proper British suspicion of those who vend salvation with impertinent enquiries after our souls. 'How is your soul today?' is not the kind of greeting or enquiry we appreciate.

We are people - I speak for myself - of moderate decencies, occasional improprieties, and sensible reciprocities. Our commitments are confused, our sacrifices domesticated, our vision intermittent. We have learnt, that is, how to conduct ourselves within acceptable limits, or at least to exhibit only what is acceptable for public scrutiny. If the lightning strikes we are equipped with lightning conductors to bring everything down to earth and restore the ordinary and *real* world of the 7.56 to Waterloo and the 9 o'clock news. C.S. Lewis called this the undeniable reality of the 73 bus.

And so the language of redemption is herded away in a safari park for overlarge ideas and wild talk, corralled off for viewing and listening on Sundays at ten - The Stag Hill half-hour. We do not care to be over-exposed to the radiation which those words carry, because they touch simultaneously on *the profoundly lamentable and the highly exalted.*

Statisticians, when they deal with a set of observations, distinguish between the full *range* and the *standard deviation.* The range covers the furthest points over which the needle can travel,

103

and the standard deviation covers the restricted area within which it usually shuttles to and fro. Redemption covers the range from top to bottom, and we - most of us - keep ourselves to the standard deviations.

'Fire!' wrote Blaise Pascal. 'At a quarter to midnight, Fire!' 'Joy, joy, tears of joy.' Good for him. But he was exceptional. John Masefield, describing Saul Kane's conversion, wrote of 'the burning cataracts of Christ'. Poet's licence no doubt. 'The burden of wickedness is intolerable,' cried Archbishop Cranmer, born 1489. Surely a bit over the top in Surrey in 1988. (We just slipped a bit on what was, after all, a very treacherous surface.) So we have carefully cut out the range of Pascal and Cranmer to stay in our standard deviation. And, we have, therefore, neither God's fear nor God's fire. 'If you have never loved you will never weep,' said John Wesley, thinking of the woman whom Jesus commended for loving much and weeping much. Weeping and loving go together like lamentation and exaltation, or captivity and liberty, or being yet a long way off and then fetched home. 'They that sow in tears shall reap in joy.'

The closest we come to this is on the screen or in singing. The real 'Chariots of Fire' are confined to the movies. 'The trumpet sounds within-a my soul' but only when we sing *about* it. Only in these projections do we get in touch with our humanity - and with our divinity. In the enlarged, enlarging world of human creativity, music or theatre, we are voyeurs of something we daily deny ourselves, and are daily denied. Our true goods have been impounded in a customs' house. How then can the evangel ever finger us? How then can our true goods ever be reclaimed?

The word 'evangel' is the same as the word 'angel' and both mean 'messenger'. The 'ev' is really 'eu' and means good, as in 'euphony' (good sound) and in 'euphoria' (good feeling). So the evangelist pouring out his redemptive talk is the one who bombards us with *good messages*. He is the finger of God trying to touch us with good tidings. He speaks not of getting us adjusted but of the wound and the salve. Those are his terms. All evangelical language is directed towards the concealed devastation. It speaks of being dead, being broken, alien, lost, sunk, enslaved, wounded, dis-eased and dis-quieted. It is looking for *trouble:* the trouble we are in that nobody knows, not even we ourselves. It names our disfigurement.

But 'they that sow in tears shall reap in joy'. Recognize the disfigurement and you recognize the transfiguration. God Himself, so proclaims the evangel, entered into the depths of the disfigurement and transformed it, *converting* that most lamentable into the highly exalted. He *reversed*, said Paul, the laws of sin and death.

But how is this reversal begun in us? Simply by 'turning'. To convert only means to turn, or to *re*-turn, or, to be turned around. As the old Shaker song says, 'It's the turning, the turning that turns out right'. About face! that's all. It means just saying 'yes' to the good spirit that moves in us all the time. The movement is towards acceptance and wholeness, power and liberty, tears and love. The Eucharist itself is no less than receptivity, meaning a turning of hearts and an opening of hands to the gifts of life. What *you* do and what *God* in His goodness does is *offer*. Everything turns on offering and then it is all yours - for the asking.

> When the Lord *turned again* the captivity of Zion then were we
> like unto them that dream
> Then was our mouth filled with laughter, and our tongue with
> joy . . .
> [For] They that sow in tears shall reap in joy.

The Work of a Deacon.
Dinner Service

'Then will I go unto the altar of God . . .'
Psalm 43:4

I want to reflect on the nature of ministry and especially on the privilege of being a deacon. The word deacon can mean a messenger, so that suggests a ministry of the word, a preaching office. But 'deacon' can also mean one who serves: a waiting man. He is appointed to be a waiting man, or one who offers service at the holy table. Before I offered that service for the first time I hardly knew the proper manners to be observed. I knew that at the holy table the priest says grace and offers grace. But I had never thought about the rules of service. So, beforehand I was instructed as to what my acceptable service might be. A colleague summarized all those rules as governed by courtesy. 'If you can't remember what to do follow the guidance offered by courtesy.' So I am reflecting on the courtesy to be exercised at the holy table, set and spread in front of us every week. How is a waiting man, and how are all who gather, waiting for food and drink, to realize the courtesy of Christ in the house of God?

If I had to say what Christianity was about I would say 'eating, drinking', and I think I would also add 'washing'. After all, why have you come here today? You come here because you need washing and because you are hungry and thirsty. The last evening of Christ was spent celebrating in the company of His friends. As He and they celebrated, the three great acts were performed: washing, eating and drinking. All that is necessary for Christianity is water for washing, bread for eating, wine for drinking. Water is clear; good to cleanse, purify, and restore. Food and drink are for sustenance, for sharing, for celebrating and making merry. What goes on at the holy table is nothing but washing and sharing out food and drink. In churches of the Catholic tradition these are the two important things to be done: Dip your hands in water. Stretch out your hands for food and for drink. Dip your *hands*, stretch out your *hands*. Christianity is about what we do with our hands and mouths: it is a hand-to-mouth religion. To live as a Christian is to live from hand to mouth.

Now I come to think about it, I have missed something out which is very important, which you also do with your hands. You may have already noticed what is missing: the fourth important act. Sometimes when kneeling where you are now, I have watched the priest using his hands. There he is, our representative, washing, taking bread and taking wine, and also doing this other action, strangely beautiful and satisfying. He raises his hands in blessing. Wash, take, give, bless. This is all the work of our hands, a miraculous kind of manual labour. Perhaps manual labour sounds odd. Not really. Everything in Christianity is work done by hand, handiwork: all of us, priests and people, work with our hands: Wash, take, give, bless. That is the acceptable service of the waiting man and of the priest.

As the ceremony of Holy Communion moves forward, passing through the phases of God's handiwork, watch carefully how you and the priests go about this manual labour. Watch the acts of cleansing and blessing. Notice how men and women go about presiding and serving at table. Notice the *hands* which put bread and wine into your *hands*. It is all a form of table service. You do it yourselves at home all the time.

As you sit at your table everyday and especially, perhaps, at meat on Sunday, the hands move backwards and forwards, passing and sharing, giving and taking. They have been washed, they clean the vessels, they handle the elements of meat and drink, they raise and offer. And as the hands give and take all along the board, we constantly give thanks. The whole of a meal has this murmur of thanks, with each act of giving and taking. Thanks; lovely; thank you; cheers. You raise your glasses or your cups in an act of common thanks and celebration. Afterwards you are all full up, fulfilled.

The priest, too, raises the cup in thanks and celebration. Watch his hand as he takes the bread, because you are all stretching out your hands when he does so. Watch him as he raises the cup, because you are all raising the cup with him. By the side of the text in the communion service there are directions about the right use of human hands: here we have a *hand*book, a manual for those things which are our proper and acceptable table service. The little book of prayer is a handbook for acceptable service at holy tables. I am going to read from my deacon's handbook: the book of our common prayer:

> There the priest is to *take* the paten *in his hands*
> And here to *lay his hand* upon all the bread.
> Here [the priest] is to *take* the Cup *into his hand*
> And here to *lay his hand* upon every vessel
> And then shall he *deliver* the same *into their hands.*

Take, lay, take, lay, deliver; wash, take, give, bless. Once those acts are done we are all *filled*, fulfilled. The end of an ordinary meal comes when we are *full* !

Fulfilment, or as the Prayer Book expresses the matter: 'fulfilled with thy grace and heavenly benediction'. The hands of the priest move, and our hands move above and along the heavenly table, to make *manifest* all the fullness of God, to pass on and show forth his plenitude. Amazingly, that word 'manifest' actually carries the secret meaning we need inside it. The glory of God is *manifest*. So what does that mean? My dictionary tells me: struck by a hand. That is the ancient root of the word *manifest*. When God is manifested to us we are struck by hand. How do the hands strike you? Are you awe-struck by the hands of God? My dictionary goes on to give the modern version of being 'struck by a hand', and says 'clearly revealed'. God, then, is clearly revealed when we are 'struck by a hand'. As the hand moves, obeying the command 'do this', we are struck by fullness, absorbed in plenitude of glory. That is why at the climax of the banquet we say, or we sing: heaven and earth are *full* of thy glory. It is as if the priest is saying through his hands that in this tiny atom which he breaks is crammed all the power of creation. As his hands fracture this microcosm the real energetic power of the universe is placed in our hands. The word is made flesh, contracted to what I can handle and see, and then exploding, expanding, repeating itself, until it fills all things.

What we handle is so tiny. The onlooker might say as the disciples said to Christ when He fed 4,000: 'From whence can a man satisfy these men with bread in the wilderness?' There is a vast emptiness, a hunger which has thousands in its grip, and a universe which is like a wilderness bereft of God and of everything which may fill and sustain us. The only answer is an act of manual labour which because it takes, breaks, blesses, and gives, makes God present as we eat and drink. The miraculous feeding in which our tiny resources are multiplied to infinity, occurs as we 'do this': take, eat, give, bless; take, lay, take, lay, deliver.

The Work of a Priest.
Re-Presenting

*'Thou wilt surely wear away . . . for this thing is too heavy for thee
. . . be thou for the people to God-ward . . . thou shalt provide out of
all the people able men . . . to be rulers . . .'*
Exodus 18:18, 19 and 21

*'. . . It is not reason that we should leave the word of God, and
serve tables . . . we will give ourselves continually to prayer,
and to the ministry of the word.'*
Acts 6:2 and 4

This might seem the perfect theme for the sociologist. It concerns, after all, the effects of the size of a community on the way tasks are distributed and defined. Our lessons offer us two cases of what sociologists describe as the division of labour and as differentiation of function. As the people of Israel multiply, Moses cannot possibly be the one and only leader and he has to delegate some of his powers and his roles to others. Similarly, as the Christian people of God become more numerous certain people have to be set aside for particular tasks. In this instance the task has to do with the fair distribution of goods, and those chosen to undertake it are seven deacons. Major matters in both cases remain to be decided at the highest level of leadership, Moses himself or the twelve apostles.

However, that is not the end of the matter. Not only is there a specialization of function which gives to the leadership the major decisions, but also one which gives to that same leadership certain religious roles. Moses has the responsibility for judging the hard cases *and* he has the responsibility of facing *Godward* on behalf of the whole people. The twelve apostles likewise have a special responsibility to be 'continually in prayer' and engaged in 'the ministry of the word'.

These developments are, of course, inevitable since in a community which has grown to any size neither its political nor its religious representatives can possibly do everything. The apostles were right to say that they could not get on with their proper task if they spent all their time on administration. No more could a Christian minister or priest today get on with his proper task if he were overwhelmed with administrative duties. If people try to do everything, making large decisions and attending to all the details, they end up distraught and very likely inefficient as well. Jethro had a firm grasp of administrative principles when he told Moses to delegate, otherwise he would 'wear away'. Jethro acts as consultant to Moses and suggests a proper reorganization and definition of tasks which will give him the freedom he needs for real leadership *and* the representation of the people before God. Moses was lucky to have this expertise within the family. Nowadays our much greater division of labour involves people who specialize in giving this kind of advice and also needing to be suitably rewarded for it.

But, however sensible these arrangements are in an expanding community, and however inevitable the division of labour may be, it involves certain dangers. These dangers have dogged the Church for all the centuries since New Testament times. One danger is the emergence of the religious specialist who does the pious bit, leaving others to concentrate exclusively on more mundane tasks. A sign that this danger is real occurs when people use the phrase 'He is going into the Church'. By the Church they mean the specialized ministry. They identify the Church with the religious specialist. The Church *means* the ordained ministry, with the rest of the Christian community tagging along as a chorus of extras. The real business of the Church is undertaken by those set aside for the priestly task, while the incidental business is performed by the laity.

This false identification of 'the Church' with its ordained representatives leads straight to the idea that one man's task is to pray, another to build, another to account, and so on. The business man goes to his office and the parson says his prayers. Of course, in one sense that is just what happens: each has a different *office*. The business man *commutes* to his office; and the priest *says* his office. The falsehood lies in the notion that something called 'the Church' can be left to look after the spiritual department while everybody else can get on with his or her own specialized interests.

It may seem absurd, but there are many people who suppose that you pay people to pray and to tend bell, book and candle, while you yourself attend to the rest of life. This is the false supposition that arises out of a quite natural division of labour and one actually suggested by the apostles themselves. Certainly the apostles did not mean that the rest of the community could safely leave the business of prayer and the word to them. Nor did they mean that a certain group of spiritually gifted people could build up treasuries of grace on which less gifted people might draw. The Church has a treasury of grace alright, but it is not a kind of stock specially invested in by those clerics set aside to run a bank of the Holy Spirit.

This division of spheres into priestly and churchly on the one hand, and secular and lay on the other, not only suits those lay people who like to leave prayer to the professionals, but it can also suit the professionals. They can gain a real but limited satisfaction from pronouncing on the things of the spirit or exercising a petty authoritarianism of the altar. (Many of the changes which have distressed lay people over recent years, including even moves in favour of participation, have been brought about by clerical manipulation.) For much of the time clergy and laity alike see certain advantages in the specialization which allows one to pray and another to ring up cash registers or sell furniture.

Yet, in spite of these dangers, what Jethro proposed to Moses and what the apostles proposed to the early Christian community was right. The apostles spoke of a special ministry of proclamation and prayer. Jethro spoke of a responsibility incumbent on Moses to represent the whole people, *Godward*. These are callings, vocations, whereby certain people might turn in the Godward direction on behalf of a whole community. All the reasonable services of the community, service at table, service across a counter, civil service, armed service, welfare and health service, needed to be taken up into their *Godward* service. All the different local responsibilities needed to be placed in the perspective provided by worship, which is the practice of prayer and the proclamation of the eternal word of law and of grace. The power to undertake this task both derives from the Christian body itself and from God: it enables the minister or priest to carry a two-way traffic, as representing God's people before God and setting forth God's word before His people. This is not to say that the traffic between God and His people may not pass any other way than an ordained ministry, since clearly some are given to be prophets, some teachers, some pastors, some evangelists. It *is* to say there is a specific privilege of representing a people Godward, thereby setting all the avocations of everyday life within the horizon of eternity.

The Godward turn is not a monopoly of those with a vocation. It does not make them the sole proprietors of channels to divinity. Their words do not even acquire any special authority. But they are appointed to make an authoritative gesture, one which gives an orientation, one which points east to the source of all being and to the great sun of righteousness. They are 'for the people . . . Godward'.

Blessed.
Good Wording

'And Isaac called Jacob, and blessed him . . .'
Genesis 28:1

'Blessed are the pure in heart: for they shall see God.'
St. Matthew 5:8

My subject concerns one word only: blessed. It is a word the monks used to love to write in their manuscripts: *'Beatus'*. It is a beautiful word but not one we use a great deal in everyday speech. If somebody sneezes we sometimes say 'bless you' to protect them, maybe against the Devil, or possibly to save them from the onset of plague or dread disease. So it can be a little piece of verbal insurance, almost word-magic. I say 'word-magic' because we are trying to bring something about by our speech. Blessing *does* somebody some good: it is a speech-*act*. When people say, as they used to, 'every blessing' they did something quite solemn by way of wishing you well. When Isaac 'blessed' Jacob he gave him the most precious and solemn thing he possessed.

People are rather sceptical about this power of speech. They used not to be. You could do good by well-wishing and you could do evil by wishing ill, through your words. There was blessing and there was cursing. You feared malediction; you sought benediction. Pronounce a blessing, pronounce a curse: there was power in pronouncements, for good or for ill. I suppose politicians, who are supposed to be practical modern men and women, are still inclined to believe in the power of cursing. Communist leaders pronounce fearful anathemas on reactionaries, imperialist running dogs and capitalist lackeys. They consign their opponents to political damnation by long ritual cursings. Still we do not think these rituals have any *real* effect. We take the view that:

Sticks and stones may break my bones
But *words* will never hurt me.

114

The same goes for blessings: words will never help me either. I think we are wrong: these good words and bad words, these benedictions and maledictions are *powerful.*

Blessings are cursings are not just words. When you curse somebody you use your body as well as your mouth. You act out the ill-will, perhaps by pointing the finger of scorn or by stabbing the air with gestures of repudiation and contempt. Perhaps a short sharp curse is accompanied by a short sharp movement of the fingers, showing you care nothing for the other person, inviting him or her to make off with due speed.

Of course, politicians are not always cursing: they spend a lot of time saying how marvellous they are, pronouncing good words on themselves. If we were not so used to this constant self-congratulation, we would think it very odd. A public figure gets up, ritually denounces his opponents as idiot incompetents, black-guards, enemies of progressive humanity, or of freedom, and then shamelessly sets himself forward as the best person, the standard-bearer of truth, of progress and sanity, the one in whom you may put your trust: sea-green incorruptible. You think a church service peculiar! It really is as odd as anything people do in Church. A leader stands on a platform, announces his own extraordinary virtues, receives extravagant plaudits from massed rows of other human beings, and finishes up by raising both his, or her, arms in the air. In the most appalling form, the leaders and the led all raise their arms and legs together declaring their almighty power and infallible rightness. And does it have no effect? On the contrary, it is power made manifest: in the boot and in the body. This is my body: this is my boot.

It is a curse, yes, a V sign to the enemy, and it is a demonstration of power: hands upraised in triumphant self-righteousness. Boot and salute. But is it a blessing? No. It is not. Politicians perform strange acts but not this strange word and this extraordinary gesture of blessing. They do almost everything else: kiss babies, salute monuments and flags, link arms in solidarity, clasp each other in a secular kiss of peace, walk in solemn procession, observe precise protocols; but they do *not* bless and they do not kneel. The clenched fist is not a blessing; the raised boots and raised arms are not benedictions. The arms and the boots are there to bring *you* to *your* knees by force.

Now, I do not want you to think there is a corrupt world of politics and an innocent world of religion. Nor do I want you to think there is a world of love which we want, and a world of power we could and should do without. I want you only to notice the difference between the political gesture and the gesture of faith. In the world of faith the knee is bent; the arm is bent. There is all the difference in the world between the stiff knee and arm and the bent knee and arm. If there is anything at all in religion it is this: the different use of the body. And why is that? Because faith uses arms and bodies to offer and receive a gift. To take in the difference just imagine what it would be like if a man of faith stood in the holy of holies and raised his arms in a gesture of political triumph, like a leader in front of a rally. Think, if in proclaiming the gift of God he stuck out his chest and held up the clenched fist or even just saluted.

That is not the way the gifts of God are made, nor is it the way the Kingdom of God comes. The gift and the Kingdom come by *blessing*. Think first of the Kingdom and remember that 'the Kingdom of God cometh not by violence'. The Kingdom is proclaimed and pronounced by words and gestures of blessing. We don't know what gesture Christ used on the Mount: it wasn't a closed fist or a salute. We do know the words were all of them benedictions.

Blessed are the poor in spirit: for theirs is the Kingdom of Heaven
Blessed are they that mourn: for they shall be comforted
Blessed are the meek: for they shall inherit the earth
Blessed are the merciful: for they shall obtain mercy
Blessed are the pure in heart: for they shall see God.

These are promises as well as blessings and benedictions. They are not a programme set before an electorate or a manifesto to be implemented if the Christian party takes power. What is promised is persecution for the sake of righteousness. The reward of being God's elect is being blessed, being comforted, obtaining mercy and seeing God. This is the true 'election'.

'To see God.' The word 'bless' is related to the word 'bliss', and that means 'joy' or 'happiness' in the sight of God. Think second, of the gift. Every Christian Eucharist is a ceremony of giving. That is what the word Eucharist means.

The cup of *blessing* which we *bless*
Is it not a sharing in the blood of Christ?

Those are St. Paul's words which are said by us all as the gift is about to be made. The blessing of the cup is a word and a gesture: a movement of mouth and hands. Just as in the political demonstration the movement of the mouths and hands makes earthly power manifest, so in this demonstration the Kingdom of God comes with power. It is a *manifestation*. What happens is not word-magic, nor is it the magic of particular movements. What becomes present is the presence and the gift. Christ is present in the blessing and in the giving.

Touched.
Shaking and Quaking

'. . . and when I heard the voice of his words, then was I in a deep sleep on my face, and my face toward the ground. And, behold, an hand touched me, which set me upon my knees . . .'
Daniel 10:9 and 10

'. . . And he laid his right hand upon me, saying unto me, Fear not; I am the first and the last.'
Revelation 1:17

Clearly, these texts are joined together by one theme: the impact of a visitation, the overpowering nature of a vision.

I think we are very prone to suppose in our heart of hearts that the Jewish prophets and the early saints of Christianity were peculiar people in more senses than one. They received heavenly messengers, entertained angels, or were taken up in the spirit into high mountains. They wrestled with the spirit, and had their hips put out of joint; they saw burning bushes and were told to take off their shoes; they saw lights and were blind for several days. Suddenly they hear cherubims and seraphims begin to cry and a burning coal is placed on their lips.

No coal has been placed on our lips; the bushes don't burn except as the sun goes down; we are not aware of entertaining angels; and we do not become disabled by wrestling in the spirit. I say that 'we' do not undergo such experiences because I think that most of us here are creatures of normality. We have those Bible people firmly segregated from our own everyday world. Saints and their visions belong to a zoo: we watch them with curiosity and amazement, behaving in their un-English biblical way, while we stay on the firm ground of ordinariness and commonsense.

Of course, we do know that sacred oddity is not quite shut up and confined in the Bible or neatly shut up in early Church history. We recognize that the lightning can strike in an English shire: Berkshire, Dorset or Surrey. The writer T.F. Powys who lived at

Chaldon near Lulworth in Dorset saw burning bushes just like Moses. Stanley Spencer the painter was always entertaining angels in Cookham. At Albury only five miles from Guildford, visionaries spoke with new tongues and expected 'the countenance divine' to shine forth on Newland's Corner. Go only a little further back and we find an English landscape alive with figures who quake or shake with local manifestations of the divine. George Fox suffered an earthquake in the spirit which threw him, bodily; and he went up on to Pendle Hill in Lancashire to sound the day of the Lord. There was a time when visionaries swarmed all over stockbroker land at St. George's Hill, Weybridge, to make real their vision of the Kingdom.

In mundane London, William Blake looked out of his window and saw the sun rising. To others he said, it was like a golden guinea; but to him it was ten thousand times ten thousand crying 'Holy! Holy! Holy!' It was William Blake who could take Bible accounts of spiritual visitation and turn them into pictures. In the Bible it speaks of the spirit passing by and the hair of our flesh rising up. So William Blake portrayed just that: the hairs rising up on the flesh. Indeed, Blake spoke of dining with Ezekiel and Isaiah, and asking them about their strange behaviour and how they could be so *sure* that God spoke to them.

So, even in commonsense England, we are not so shut off from visitations as we sometimes suppose. But when remarkable things happen we don't fall over, or go dumb, or quake, or go into a swooning sleep. Instead we use language which talks *about* all those things. We say, for example:

Honestly, I was quite thrown.

I was knocked all of a heap.

It came to me in a blinding flash.

It left me *dumbfounded*.

I was quite lost for words.

Thrown, knocked, blinded; deprived of speech; lost for breath or for words. Spiritual experience is what *throws us*.

That brings us back straightaway to these texts. They are all about being 'thrown' and hurled to the ground. The glory appears to Ezekiel and he is instantly prone, face downward. Daniel looks

119

up and sees 'a certain man', his face 'as the appearance of lightning' and the lightning strikes him face down on the earth. John the Divine on the Isle of Patmos sees the *I am*, the Amen, Alpha and Omega, and a man shining like the sun. In a moment he is prostrate, as though dead. The message is quite plain. When you 'see the light', or the sun in its strength, you lose all your *self*-possession and are completely *thrown*, quite *speechless*. Mary herself when she saw the visiting angel was 'troubled at his saying and cast in her mind what salutation this might be'.

There seem to be similar things here in all these experiences: an onset, a loss of capability, and a sense of being raised up. Moreover, the people who are visited are entirely ordinary and wonder how this could happen to them, of all people. They feel an almost physical pressure driving them *down* before they can respond. As we say 'it *came* to me'. Mary didn't walk out looking for angels, but the angel of the Lord knocked imperiously at her heart, saying 'Hail'. *Angelus ad Virginem inquit 'Ave'.* Jeremiah was known by God, he says, even before he was formed in the belly, and ordained before he came out of the womb. Which is to say: it was all *there* long before this terrible ordination occurred.

And then there is this strange incapacity. The chosen are incapable and they know it. Moses is a stammerer anyway; Jeremiah says he is only a mere child. Samuel *is* a child. This incapacity is necessary. The Lord's rebuke is precisely this: you must know that you are ordained in other strengths than those you already offer. Jeremiah, Zacharias, and Mary in their different ways, all almost try to turn aside or at least wonder how anything could come about through them. Jeremiah says, 'I cannot speak; for I am a child.' But the Lord put forward His hand and touched His mouth. Isaiah too felt the fire pressed against his lips. Zacharias, told of an unbelievable birth to his wife Elizabeth, is dumb with surprise. The others in the temple knew Zacharias had seen something because 'he beckoned unto them, and *remained speechless*.'. The birth of John the Baptist comes to querulous, speechless Zacharias and to Elizabeth: 'she that was called barren'. And Mary, too, said, 'How shall this be . . .?'

The child who doesn't know what to say, the stammerer, the one with the unclean lips, the querulous, the barren, and one who is no more than a handmaid: they receive the unexpected visitor. Each one of them is told: you can stand, you can speak, through you it comes to birth. It is *laid* on them. 'Lo, *this* hath touched thy lips,' says the seraphim to Isaiah. 'Stand upon thy feet and *I* will speak to thee,' says the Lord to Ezekiel. 'Stand upright ... greatly beloved ... and understand the words,' said the voice to David. 'Write,' said the first, and the last and living one to John. To Mary the messenger said, 'The Power of the Highest shall *overshadow* thee.' 'Behold the handmaid of the Lord; be it unto me according to thy Word.'

That might seem to be conclusion enough. We could say 'Amen' and stop. It is sufficient to recount the form which visitation takes. We might think we are being invited to go charismatic. If so, we could turn all our life and worship into this sense of being visited and thrown. We could think that anyone who claims to have been thrown off balance has received a true message.

As human beings, framed in the divine image, we live by reason, order and purpose. That means this invitation from the visitor must be scrutinized with all our powers. What follows is not continuous indulgence in the moment of disclosure. That solves nothing and takes us nowhere. There are so many spiritual stillbirths precisely because we become fixated on the announcement, lost in simply repeating the creative moment.

We are called rather to this scrutiny. The visitors as often come from dark regions of chaos and destruction as from the height of order and love. Humankind must monitor the message, or as St. Paul puts it 'test the spirits, whether they be of God'. The demons enter at the same door as the angels, and throw us permanently off balance, divert us and especially they divert us with the pure deliciousness of the wound, offering us permanent death, an endlesss indulgent swoon or sleep of the spirit. People entertain demons unawares as easily as they entertain angels.

So in speaking and in obeying what we owe the light is a direction and a lucidity; direction of the will and lucidity of mind. What follows the disclosure and the visitation is *ordering*. Each one of us in the ordinariness of our lives encounters the visit, which comes to us uninvited. But such lights as come to us point precisely to a long scrutiny of self and mind. Between the unsought announcement and the final vision comes the lucidity of mind and will. Any light we have demands this: ordering, scrutiny, lucidity, all those things without which the announcement slips back, null and void, into devilry, confusion and destruction.

Enlightened.
Lucidity and Illumination

'[God] . . . who only hath immortality, dwelling in the light . . .'
I Timothy 6:16

Reading this text I reflect on the nature of light and how we use
light to speak about God. We respond to light as one of the primary
signatures of the divine. We use the sign of light to indicate God's
presence and to speak of His nature. The language of light and of
illumination and lucidity is the universal speech of divinity. So I
want to survey the range of this universal speech, from the light
that is in creation to the illumination that comes in the soul.

Light is God's initial creation; it is the first-born element of
His creative power. God spoke light into being: 'Let there be light,
and there was light'. So we accord to light a primacy in the order
of things. Light is like God Himself because without its presence
nothing can exist physically or grow biologically. The efflores-
cence of light is the precondition of the emergence of life.

Indeed, in the divine 'sign language', light and day go with
growth and life, just as darkness goes with death. Death belongs
to the valley of the shadow. The dying go into the dark and into
eternal night. Night signifies a changelessness in which nothing
stirs. Of course, there is a mystical counterpoint to this in which
night is not only negation and obscurity but protection and
mystery: 'There is in God, some say, a deep, but dazzling darkness'. That is one of the greatest lines in English mystical poetry.
But still the primary significance of light is life and of darkness,
death.

Night also lies next to the blackness in which nothing can be
discerned or distinguished. And, moving along our chain of
meaning that links light with perception and clarity, day brings
clarification. In the light we are able to see clearly. That refers not
only to our perception of the visible world, but to the way wisdom

and understanding 'dawn on us'. Physical perception shades into spiritual enlightenment. At one level we apprehend the physical world because it is suffused with light; at another level we comprehend the human and spiritual world because our understanding has been enlightened. Once we were blind 'but now we see'. 'Lighten our darkness we beseech thee, O Lord.' We say that prayer at evening, but we are asking not for physical sight but for spiritual *in*-sight. So we make a transition from the outward light to the inward light and to the fanning of the divine spark within the soul. That spark represents our rational faculty in which scripture sees 'the candle of the Lord', and it represents our whole spiritual being. It is within that inner secret chamber of our selves that the candle of the Lord may burn with the radiance of lucidity and illumination. *Dominus illuminatio mea*: the Lord is my light. As physical light is to physical life so this spiritual and rational enlightenment is to our spiritual being.

And, once again, darkness signifies the contrast: the powers of darkness and the prince of darkness designate the realm of evil and nothingness. To live in the light is to find footholds on the path to goodness; to be lost in darkness is to lose all footing and fall prey to the demonic and to self-destruction. Those who seek the light 'cast away the works of darkness'.

So, then, as we survey the range of meanings in this language of light, we see how it signifies all the physical and spiritual good of our outer and inner worlds and how darkness signifies chaos, negativity and evil. Light clarifies and enlightens and gives life to body and spirit; darkness obscures, leaving us blind, lost, confused, and lifeless. The Bible itself turns around that dramatic contrast; and it is a call for us to become the children of the light, and sons and daughters of the morning. It celebrates the primal light of physical genesis and it seeks the light of spiritual truth. The prologue of Genesis and the prologue of St. John's gospel are twin hymns to outward and inward light.

God *is* the fount of life and light and we are to seek that immortal fountain. We are not dealing just in a dramatic contrast but in a *process* and *movement* towards the fountain of all light and love. The process can be expressed in all the imagery of illumination, the discovery of the fountain, the slow movement of the dawn. It is an historical journey and a personal journey. It is historical because humankind has stumbled towards the light through time, and it is personal because each individual seeks the light of life. There is an advent in history and an advent in our personal experience. We are as those 'who watch for the morning'.

'The people that walked in darkness have seen a great light.' That is an historical enlightenment. 'The Sun of Righteousness rises with healing in his wings.' That is also an enlightenment of self. The key image here is of rising and arising. We are to awake and to rise from the dead. As Gerard Manley Hopkins put it: 'Let him *easter* in us' - meaning by that: let him be our dayspring and our daystar, our light and our east. Let him cancel our evil and rend our entombment. It is all summed up in Charles Wesley's hymn:

Christ, whose glory fills the skies,
Christ, the true, the only light.
Sun of Righteousness arise,
Triumph o'er the shades of night
Day-spring from on high, be near,
Day-star in my heart appear.

Awake O thou that sleepest and rise from the dead and Christ shall give thee light.

Harmony.
Clash and Resolution

*'Praise him with the sound of the trumpet: praise him with the psaltery
and harp. Praise him with the timbrel and dance: praise him with
stringed instruments and organs.'*
Psalm 150 :3 and 4

*'Blessed Cecilia, appear in visions
To all musicians, appear and inspire:
Translated Daughter, come down and startle
Composing mortals with immortal fire.'*
W.H. Auden. From 'Anthem for St. Cecilia's Day'

I have two texts; one nearly three thousand years old, the other not much over forty years old. The first is from Psalm 150 and the second is from W.H. Auden's 'Anthem for St. Cecilia's Day'.

November 22 is the day of St. Cecilia, patroness of music and musicians, whom tradition generously credits with the invention of the organ. To tell the truth, the connection between the Cecilia who was martyred in Sicily around 176 AD and music is obscure almost to the point of extinction. This doesn't much matter, because her name simply gives us an opportunity to celebrate the divine art of music, and, I may say, to thank our own musicians for what they do for our worship here. Certainly it is proper to remember her today since it was in 1683 that the remembrance of St. Cecilia was brought from France to England and celebrated with three odes in her honour, all with music composed by Henry Purcell.

Music was the latest of all the arts to ripen. The miracle of music such as we know today was first wrought in Notre Dame almost exactly seven hundred years ago. That was a strange and marvellous spring time which entered an early summer of genius in the sixteenth century. It is music from that early summer which we most often hear in cathedrals: Lassus and Palestrina, Byrd and

Tallis. Since that time music has been the most pure and untrammelled expression of the human spirit. It is a glorious mathematics in which we hear the numerical structure of the universe freely translated by sound.

Mathematicians often tell us about the beauty of number and the singular pleasure of thinking God's thoughts after Him. What we hear in music is a kind of transubstantiation of ratio and proportion. What the mathematician knows by intellect is recreated by the composer and by the performer in golden numbers: the numerical tables of the heart. Sir James Jeans, the physicist, argued for just this special relationship between numbers and notes.

These are large claims. Music is not just a sensuous tickling of the ear but a reworking of elements which are already given in the nature of things. When the sounds of music vibrate the air and travel through the human ear, they obey certain rules of regularity, i.e. symmetry, balance, stress, beat and proportion. When the composer masters these rules, working out his free mathematics, we experience something which we can only call 'authority'. Once the musician has mastered the ground rules he seeks for combinations and recombinations which we recognize as fully achieved, perfectly realized, authoritative. Musical masters write as 'men having authority'. That is why we call them 'masters'. For a similar reason the true performance carries its own authority and sense of mastery.

The elements of music are as mysterious as anything we know in ordinary science. If you go to your piano and touch only one note, say, the C below middle C, the sounds will divide and subdivide until they give you the complete scale. The many are contained in the one. If you walk up the scale, you experience a strange satisfaction, because here you move from rest to unrest and back to rest again. If you touch just three notes, C, E, and G, you have a common chord, which is in a state of perfect rest, needing nothing added. Simply to hear this perfect relationship has been for some people a revelation. When Albert Schweitzer first heard that chord as a child he fainted with shock. Robert Browning wrote of 'the C Major of this life', meaning something perfect and all-inclusive, the point of rest from which everything begins and to which everything returns.

When you use words like that you see how we approach a theology *already in* music. There is the great originator, the single point out of which the whole ladder or scale emerges and then revolves, following its inner nature, into an infinity of musical worlds. There is the ladder itself, the scale moving through all the compass of the notes from the first point of rest to the last point of rest: C to C.

There is a chord, perfect and all inclusive, needing nothing outside itself, which then modulates and shifts to other chords which are needy, tense, incomplete, demanding to move to the point where the tension is released and resolved. If I were to stop on one of them, part way through a sequence, you would say to me, 'You can't leave it there.' The music has to travel through what is restless back to the point of origin. Some music moves by clash and resolution, clash and resolution, suspending the hearer through sequence after sequence up to an overwhelming point of climax, which then breaks off and returns to a final restatement. Sometimes music will travel far away from its origin, as if bearing almost no relation to the ground from which it took off, and then slowly it finds its way back to source.

This return after a long journey is a kind of satisfaction corresponding to the needy, imperfectly resolved tensions through which we have passed. Or, alternatively, the music states the basic elements in all their simplicity as if affirming: this is *so*; it is *thus*.

Let me give examples of frustration and release. In the third movement of Beethoven's Fifth Symphony the music turns serpentine, trying to push its way through, stopping, twisting back on itself. Finally, as if exhausted, it pulsates on C alone, waiting while strange ghostly figures begin to shift around that underlying pulse, probing with more and more tense and frustrated expectation. Then the barrier breaks, the darkness dissolves in a white sheet of overwhelming light, which leaps through the common chord and then triumphantly returns down the scale to C once more.

Beethoven says it over and over again: see, here is the basic structure of things now arranged in triumphal sequences which no bedevillment can deny, overturn or render imperfect. The only words which might match such sounds would be those of faith: god of gods, light of light, very God of very God. As he concludes his symphony, Beethoven iterates and reiterates what is nothing else than the solemn chord of C, but with a sense of the Omega, the first and the last.

At other times this overwhelming sense of having come through to the blazing unity of the perfect chord is pared down to pure contemplation. Beethoven here is not triumphant so much as contemplating a slow opening out and opening up of a new heaven and a new earth. In the last movement of his last sonata, he returns again to this C major, but now in a condition of complete simplicity. His music has explored everything and now he will say something again, yes, say it again, which could not be simpler and which has unanswerable authority. This is nothing less than beatitude: a realm of inviolate completion built upon that which *is*. Over and over in his music, Beethoven has returned to a restful, almost hidden song, and as he comes to reveal and unveil this *last* song he writes above it: 'slowly, simply and singing'. It is, as Wilfred Mellers has said, a reconciliation of everything that has gone before: you may call it all-sufficient grace. The body is suspended; everything is held in a movement which has almost passed beyond time to pure statement; the still point of the turning world. This is the moment when you know that: All shall be well and all manner of things shall be well.

When I was training to be a musician my teacher used to say: let the music *breathe*. I want to conclude by saying something about the *breath* of music. There are at least two aspects to 'breathing' in music. You have to submit yourself to an inner pulse and let it alone. There must be no forcing, pushing, or trying to impose your own view. The world of the spirit, especially where the spirit is whole and holy, is like that. You do not seek it or play it up, but only *allow* it to breathe. Everything is already *there*, if you only consent to let it be. In that last hidden song of Beethoven you can only 'let be'. You are not playing the music, because the music is playing you. There is a pulse there which corresponds both to your own heart beat and to mathematical proportion. The key is found in pulsation: a truth *about your body and about the world* to which you must submit if you are to enter into this joy at the heart of men and things.

The other aspect of breath is *pressure*. The word 'spirit' means 'breath', and both your breath and the outside world depend on *pressure*. Just as you must accept the pulse so you must find that 'correct pressure'. When you submit to that which presses upon you then you are 'inspired'. All the great musicians spoke of this pressure upon them, which is then realized in composition. This is an 'I yet not I, but the spirit of God which worketh in me'. We say of such things that they suddenly 'come' to us, by a kind of gift. We speak of people as having 'gifts'. The gift that the musician has, in the creation of sounds, is not only self-manufactured by training and discipline, but 'God-given'. These gifts allow man to be in the image of God, confronting the original simplicity, and out of that moving into an infinity of worlds, evolving and expanding beyond all we can know or think.

Humankind has this 'gift' to exercise within a small compass of a chant or a large compass of a symphony. If we take only the small compass of the chant we sing to the psalms, we have before us at least fifty million combinations. If we take works of a larger scale the number expands to infinity. So we have here something which allows us to participate in Godhead, because we engage in the imitation of God. Through the travail and the constraints imposed by those laws which govern God's creation, and our own creativity, there can emerge a manifestation of the highest energy. What we have then is not some idea about God, but a real presence: being in itself and for itself. Browning said that all we have dreamed of good shall exist, not its semblance, but itself. Music takes us to the edge of *that*.

Music.
Social and Personal

'Moses verily was faithful in all his house, as a servant . . . .
But Christ as a son . . .'
Hebrews 3 : 5 and 6

This text is built around a contrast between Moses and Christ. That contrast is, of course, also between the Old Testament and the New, between Judaism and Christianity. On the one hand we have a religion of the social covenant. Because it is social it is built around authority, justice and law. It is represented by kings and judges, and by prophets of social justice. On the other hand, we have a religion of the personal covenant. Because it is personal it is built around sin and grace, birth, death and resurrection. It is represented by the man, Jesus, who was born, who 'died once unto sin, and who liveth for ever unto God'.

Now I want to take that fundamental contrast and work it out in relation to two of the greatest figures of musical history, George Frederic Handel and Johann Sebastian Bach. This may seem an odd procedure, but it is appropriate for two reasons. One reason is that 1985 marks the tercentenary of the birth of both composers. The other reason is that this coming week contains the feast of St. Cecilia, patron saint of music. Never again will it be so natural and appropriate to preach on these two great composers as embodying a contrast between the old dispensation and the new. Inevitably, such a contrast is not complete. I must neglect Handel the master of mood, motive and human passion in his forty operas. Moreover, Handel in his 'Messiah' and in 'Theodora' brought sublime illumination to the Christian themes of martyrdom, death, and immortality. And Bach was, from time to time, a composer who complimented his prince by offering him a birthday cantata, for example, and who composed sociable music for the entertainment of his

131

neighbour. But the difference remains between a great artist who celebrated the social and the temporal and a great artist who sought after the personal, mystical and eternal. The one was more outward, the other more inward.

Part of the achievement of Handel was to bring a Greek spirit to the Old Testament and to rework ancient Greece and ancient Israel in the context of eighteenth-century Britain. That fitted the spirit of the times very well, because many Britons were reshaping their landscape after classical models, and they were also shaping their national history as though Britain were a second Israel. Eighteenth-century Britons saw themselves as a covenant nation, chosen by God for His providential purposes. They received His blessings and were, occasionally, attentive to His warnings. Handel's Englishmen became attached to the this-worldly tone of the Old Testament; they admired its idea of collective action symbolized by a king who led his people on the basis of a divine covenant. In the Old Testament they could read about commerce, prosperity, territorial expansion, competitive nationalism and the search for political autonomy; and all these things mirrored their own vision of England's vocation. The ancient Jews were people of the law; they belonged to what the epistle to the Hebrews calls 'the house of Moses'. So, many Englishmen thought, did they. (Perhaps this is one reason why English religion faltered when the god of battles failed them in 1914.)

So, when Handel composed his magnificent work 'Israel in Egypt', which begins with the first words of our Old Testament lesson, and which celebrates the liberation of the Jewish people, the English were prepared to see themselves writ large. When Handel wrote 'Judas Maccabbaeus' they knew he was writing about contemporary Britain. The Maccabbees died for the 'law', that is, for the ancestral faith of their people. 'See the Conquering Hero comes' celebrated the victories of Judas Maccabbaeus and victorious England. When Handel set 'O lovely peace with plenty crowned' with its references to fleecy flocks adorning the hills, the English who heard him saw both the landscape of the psalmist and the green hills of England.

Nor was this necessarily an ignoble vision: like Americans the English saw themselves as a covenant people and as 'one nation under God'. The vehicle of this vision was found in great ceremonies carried by a priesthood of high estate and centred on the Royal house. It was found also in dramatic figures who rose to heroic leadership. As Paul Lang has put it:

> No one in their entire history has realised for the English these ideals, these thrilling ceremonies, these dramatic figures, with more conviction, more majesty and grandeur, and more exhilarating immediacy than Handel in his anthems and oratorios.

That is why the anointing of the King is always accompanied by 'Zadok the Priest', why the Royal wedding concluded with 'Let the bright Seraphim' and it is even why the body of Mrs. Gandhi was followed by the dead march in 'Saul'. The public, the civic, the sense of jubilant community in a covenant nation, the respect for law, are all raised to transcendence in the music of Handel. On the one side is the Authorised Version viewed, in Huxley's words, as the national epic; on the other side is that great text raised to the power of universal genius.

Of course, that is not the whole of religion, however important it has been in the Jewish, English, American and other traditions, and it is not the whole of Handel. In the 'Messiah' we have a turning towards the luminous advent of God made man, the laceration of the despised and rejected saviour, and a faith that 'as in Adam all die, even so in Christ shall all be made alive'. Indeed, in his 'Theodora' Handel touches the ultimate note of spiritual security and inner stillness before the mysteries of self-giving and immortality.

But it is chiefly in Bach that we come to the gospel and the mystery of Christ. Bach's music centres around the hope of His coming, His birth, His death, resurrection and ascension. It is also centred in the Christian community rather than in the city or the nation. Bach fixes his eye on Christ and on His cross. Indeed, the suffering God is the key that unlocks his music: sometimes the music is even written in the form of a cross. The notes are lacerated, torn and suspended, almost bearing up the body of the saviour. They have a dying fall.

This means that the world of Bach moves between the poles of sin and grace, abasement and joy. In his mass, he begins by approaching God in profound humility, conscious of the sin that separates man from peace. Man must pass through tribulation and abasement before he attains everlasting joy and felicity. The music for the *Crucifixus* hangs suspended in deep mourning; it plumbs the depths of Christ's suffering until the sounds flower in radiant joy. Yet after the painful suspensions of crucifixion, the music leaps upward to affirm the resurrection and the life. The *Sanctus* is ablaze with holy threes to celebrate the Triune God. The upper voices swing like a huge censer, while the bass moves through the whole range of the scale. The perfect number circles above the complete scale.

At the heart of Bach's music is a personal apprehension of the presence of Christ. In a simple chorale like 'Jesu, joy of man's desiring' Christ is the summit of joy and the source of all peace. The music flows with unbroken continuous peace. There is a sense of sweetness whenever Bach writes of Christ. The strings surround Christ's words with an aura of beauty and power. For Bach, Christ is the bridegroom of the Advent, the beloved one of the Song of Songs. He is the one who steals upon the soul, who gives benediction in his miraculous birth, who comes again and again with glory. The heart of Bach, and of his music, dances at His name.

Throughout his life, Bach played with the sacred numbers: one and three, seven and twelve. His setting of the words 'And was incarnate of the Virgin Mary' is exactly forty nine bars long: seven times seven. In his last years he took a Christmas hymn and wove music around it to demonstrate the mathematical perfection of divine order and proportion. The Christmas hymn 'Von Himmel Hoch' ('From Heaven above to Earth I come') is a song of the utmost joy and simplicity which Bach surrounds with traceries which move one inside the other at different speeds in perfect equilibrium. It is pure ingenuity at play before God within the disciplines of musical art. At the very end, Bach tucks in the musical equivalent of his own name B-A-C-H. It is, therefore, his own musical offering. The human donor of the divine message is one Johann Sebastian Bach. Bach has become the human means whereby God's gift is made manifest; the gift of the spirit in music, the gift of Himself in the new-born Christ.

Peace: 1.
The Price of Peace

'And your feet shod with the preparation of the gospel of peace.'
Ephesians 6 : 15

'Grant . . . to thy faithful people pardon and peace.'
Collect for Trinity 21 (Book of Common Prayer)

These texts both refer to peace: the one speaks of the gospel of peace and the other prays that all faithful people may receive pardon and peace. I want to think about peace, starting from the way the 'peace movement' demonstrates against further instalments of weapons of war. When Beethoven wrote his great commentary on the Christian Eucharist, he concluded with a strange almost military movement: *Dona, Dona, Dona nobis pacem.* It was a demand, almost a peace march, with trumpets blaring: *Give* us, *give* us, *give* us peace. Above the score are the words 'A prayer for outward *and* for inward peace'.

So there are two kinds of peace, inward and outward. Like Beethoven we all want both peace in the world and a peace which the world cannot give. The Bible speaks of a civic and universal peace, when all spears have become pruning hooks: and also of another peace established in the depths of the human heart. I want, first, to think about that outer peace. The Bible offers us pictures of it. We are shown Jerusalem, the city girt about with praise, and we are asked to pray for her peace. 'Peace be within thy walls and prosperity within thy palaces.' 'Pray for the peace of Jerusalem. They shall prosper that love thee.' The city is full of merchandise and bustle: a multitude of dromedaries and camels. By contrast there are the ravages of war and occupation. 'How doth the city sit solitary that was full of people! . . . The ways of Zion do mourn . . . Jerusalem, Jerusalem!'

These simple and powerful images are about outward peace and the terror of war and servitude. This is the human condition:

moments of peace and liberty surrounded by times of war, misery and slavery. The Jews, like human beings in every age, looked for some way through the dreadful impasse, which might bring about a stable and lasting peace.

One way, followed by the overwhelming majority of the human race, is the way of Judas Maccabbaeus, and the way of the revolts of 70 AD and 135 AD. Often it did not work. The last revolt ended in the destruction of Jerusalem in which 'not one stone was left upon another'. Sometimes it did work for a while and many Jews saw the Maccabbaean revolt as the final issue between the rule of God and the rule of man. But the triumph turned out only temporary.

The other path through the impasse is by exemplary suffering: acceptance of the conqueror's will. This is a way which can be taken only by dedicated groups or by individual people. It offers a witness against destruction and it is ready for sacrifice in the cause of peace. Hardly ever has a nation attempted such an act of collective atonement. Usually the suffering servants of God have been driven helplessly to sacrifice only because there was no alternative. The holocaust forty years ago left one mark: never again would Jews go as sheep to the slaughter. Today the new Israel remembers that terrible trauma and is willing to turn her pruning books into weapons of war.

The human story, then, is one of wars and rumours of wars without end. It is a long Passchendaele of horror: 16,000 recorded conflicts. We read a tale of blood. Faith has tried to encompass this bloodiness, seeking to see if anything can redeem the loss, to place all our meaningless Passchendaeles in the light of Christ's death and passion.

I think of two ways in which artists have tried to do so. You can find them in two chapels. One is a vast glass and steel edifice in the centre of the American Air Force Base at Colorado Springs. Inside, over the altar, is a strange and fearsome sign, which sums up in its tortuous shape the paradox of war and peace. As you enter you think first it is a plane ascending, then you see that it is a dove descending, and finally you realize it is also a cross. The message is: the plane ascends in order to ensure that the dove of peace descends. Without power there is no peace, but power must be dedicated to peace. The fact that the plane and dove are also a cross places all our Passchendaeles in the context of the Passion. But, of course, that is an idealization: a necessary but misleading half truth. Power is only sometimes directed to peace; the passion of men is often just spilt blood for no reason whatever beyond aggrandizement and state interest.

The other chapel is very tiny. You can find it tucked away in the Berkshire Downs at Burghclere. It is a memorial to the First World War by Stanley Spencer. He sets his passion in Macedonia. The focus is a huge mural above the altar of Christian sacrifice. This mural shows a multitude of crosses, which the resurrected soldiers give to Christ as symbols of their passion. In other pictures the soldiers are engaged in their ordinary duties: small ordinary human things, and Spencer himself is included picking up litter with a bayonet. There are different forms of understanding here. To pick up litter is to see a revelation in mundane, disagreeable duties: 'heaven in a grain of sand'. But the central concern is the redemption of an intolerable horror, a transmutation of suffering. By this means, said Spencer, I 'redeemed my experience and recovered my self'.

But in the search for outward peace, there is, in the end, a blockage which cannot be removed: there seems no way through that evades the tortuous union of the plane, the dove and the bloody sacrifice. What then of inner peace? Holy scripture and Christian worship are full of a quest for inward peace which is also, of course, a peace with the brethren. As the disciples sit in fear behind closed doors, the living Christ comes among them and says, 'Peace be with you.' The blessings we offer include the gift of peace: 'And now the God of peace . . .', 'May the peace of God, which passeth all understanding, keep your hearts and minds in the knowledge and love of God'. Men and women pray for 'peace at the last'.

Inner peace is something which is *offered* and something we *find*. Peace comes to us; and yet we go looking for it. Whenever we talk of peace we include these two things: the gift of it, and the long search for it. 'Grant us thy peace,' we say, or 'Somehow I must *find* some peace'. There is always the gift and the search.

They seem to be contrasted. In the one case you are there and then the message of peace is just offered. It comes almost when you are not looking. Most of my own life is quite turbulent and fragmented and then an avenue of peace is disclosed. The gift of peace is hidden and then quite unexpectedly it is uncovered. Something emerges inside us which we could describe as 'pure and peaceable wisdom'. It is as if we are surrounded by unseen messengers and guides: presences, which make themselves known and can lead us beside the still waters.

Yet, peace is also the conclusion of a long search. We must *prepare* for peace, *seek* after peace. All our lives we are *looking* for peace. *Prepare, seek, look.* We will travel a long way for even a bit of peace. So there is both a standing still when we are surprised by a gift and there is this long trying to find the things which belong to our peace.

Inner peace is not finally achieved without exacting its own terrible price. Jeremiah speaks of a peace which is no peace because the hurt is healed '*too slightly*'. We may apply what placebos we may but we do not touch the deep hurt corrupting and clouding the whole soul. The hurt must be totally entered into and *then* taken away.

To fully accept this hurt and, therefore, to bear it away is *spiritual* warfare. The hurt exacts blood and death: in seeking inner peace the passion cannot be avoided. The search for inner, as for outward peace, is passionate: sacrificial. The divine in man, God in Christ, probes the hurt and takes it fully into and upon himself. The surgeon absorbs the wound. The depth and horror of man's hurt is placarded, held up for us in the broken body.

This is the Lamb's battle for peace. There can be no avoidance and no easy cure of souls. The wound must be probed to its depths and the pain accepted. Before we can say 'Grant us thy peace' we must say first 'O Lamb of God, that taketh away the sins of the world'.

What we celebrate in the Eucharist is this: life through death and peace through the war of the Lamb. 'For with his stripes we are healed; the chastisement of our peace was upon Him.' That is why this ceremony of healing, this offer of new life, this proclamation of peace, is contained in this and only this, 'the blood of Christ . . . the body of Christ'.

The fifteenth-century Scottish Franciscan poet says it for us all:

Done is the battle on the dragon black
Our champion Christ confounded has his force
The gates of hell are broken with a crack
The sign triumphal raised is of the cross
The devils tremble with hideous voice
The souls are ransomed and to their bliss can go
Christ with his blood our ransom doth endorse
Surrexit Dominus de sepulchro.

Prayer.
Spiritual Flexitime

'. . . he shall come unto us as the rain . . .'
Hosea 6:3

I want to focus on something I don't know enough about. That
something is prayer. To be quite truthful, I know so little about
prayer because I don't actually do enough praying. And I don't
pray because I don't have much spare time. There is always a long
list of things I have to do, and the moment spare time emerges I
take the first thing on the list and fill up my spare time. I have been
doing this now for years, if not decades. I do not even have the time
to observe what it is I am actually doing at the moment I am doing
it. Because, you see, I am so intent on the business of getting it *done*.
My life consists of tasks: today I have this and this and this to get
done, and that is true even of quite pleasant things like meeting a
colleague for tea. He, or she too, is part of my rota, the wheel of
duties on which my life can inexorably turn. If I were to set aside
proper time for prayer it would be one more spike on that wheel
of duties - and now, I suppose, I had better get my praying *done*.

I went to a cardiologist and he made two comments. First of
all, he said, 'Why is your heart protesting?' Second, he diagnosed
me as suffering from 'conceptual overload': too many things
jostling at the same narrow entrance so that none get through.
'Conceptual overload' is precisely that: a kind of pressure that
builds up in your head and in the end builds up round your heart.

So, he proposed some meditative exercises. In short, he
prescribed some secular prayer time. The trouble was that these
exercises ended up on the spike of things to be done, another item
in the in-tray, another addition to conceptual overload. It was bad
enough having to read the articles in my own line of academic
business without reading *his* articles on conceptual overload.

Once he asked me what *I* thought the problem was, and I said it had to do with the nature of time, which brought a quick quizzical look and no further comment. Doctor's surgeries are no place to discuss the nature of time, and in any case he was a very busy man himself with precious little time to think about time. I wasn't surprised he had to see another patient. His rota turned, and in came the next person.

That fragment of autobiography is the story of a lot of our lives, not only mine, and I introduce it simply because it helps me say something about prayer. Prayer is, in the first place, the finding of a space and the displacement and abandonment of the rota. It actually requires not just *a* place or *a* space, but a different approach to the whole relentless schedule of tasks. To pray is not to fit some prayer in alongside all those other engagements, but it is to stop *still* in your tracks. Prayer is to allow yourself to be pulled up short. Prayer is not *a place* in your diary of daily engagements, but a query mark placed against your whole schedule and the priorities which govern that schedule.

Prayer, in short, *is* stillness and spaciousness. It requires that you look up from what you are doing in order to re-view your life. It offers perspectives which set your pressing priorities on the horizon of eternity. That is why Christ Himself went up into a mountain to pray, because there the perspectives were altered and things settled in their appropriate place.

So, then, the first thing about prayer is the making of a space. In that space you have to learn how to breathe. That may have something to do with your physical breathing, because the rhythm of your breath is related to the rhythm of your inner life. When we are anxious we catch our breath; when we breathe quietly and slowly something begins to emerge within us which is content and reposeful. We recover the sense of repose, and we begin to pass beneath the surface flurry and fury of our lives. The Bible speaks of the knowledge that comes with stillness: be still and *know*. If you let *go* you can let yourself *be*.

Once we are still and open to a new knowledge of ourselves and to a re-view of our world, we are then in a condition of listening. We are in touch and open. Prayer, then, is this being in touch and this openness. Because of the constant pressure of the daily overload, all the entrances of our being are battened down and to pray is to unfold. Usually we are bent double with our sense of care, so to pray is to unbend and let go the burden of care. You are losing your burden, some upper self, and gaining your own unburdened soul. When that happens you are able to *attend*.

That may mean that you pay attention to the world and recover the sense of miracle in all things it offers. It also means recovering the sense of miracle in yourself. You go *out* to the world and *in* to yourself. You are now in a condition of simplicity and of faithfulness of spirit and of wholeness. Previously you were full of dis-ease and un-ease, and now you are made whole again. To be made whole again is to be saved. When you pray you simply open up the path to salvation.

It is as we recover this wholeness and this faithfulness of spirit that we can appropriate the words of scripture very simply as the pathways along which others have passed seeking the same wholeness. A wise and lucid spiritual guide, Gerard Hughes, suggests that we let the words of scripture enter our minds not as descriptions of past events but as present realities of our spiritual condition. He says we must open ourselves to them not as print, out there, but as words coming from the mystery of our own being. That is what prayer is: a welling up of the mysteries of our being. Read (say) Hosea that way and it is a prayer for torn and dry roots to be healed and renewed by the coming of the rain. It was Hosea's journey and it can be ours.

> Come, and let us return unto the Lord: for he hath torn and he will heal us; he hath smitten and he will bind us up. Then shall we *know* if we follow on to *know the Lord*; his going forth is prepared as the morning: and he shall come unto us as the rain, as the latter and former rain to the earth.

> Lord, send my roots rain.

Peace: 2.
God's Rule

'And let the peace of God rule in your hearts . . .'
Colossians 3:15

So far as I know there is no definitive Christian doctrine of peace.
I have taken the precaution of looking up a reputable dictionary
of theology and peace does not appear at all. Perhaps it is just as
well that a doctrine of peace has not been set forth since there
would almost certainly have been a war about it, with all the
partisans of a true Christian doctrine of peace resolutely hacking
to pieces the defenders of a heretical doctrine. And vice-versa.
(Happily, doctrines of peace have been left to secular philosophies.
Nineteenth-century liberals had a doctrine of peace and the
conditions under which it was obtainable; and so have twentieth-
century Marxists. And their rival doctrines of the road to peace fill
our world with their bellicose clangour. They both believe that the
rival doctrine of peace is bound up with a social system which
leads to war; and they are ready to beat each other over the head
to prove their point.)

All the same it is strange that we have no such doctrine. Think
of the number of times the word comes in the Bible: 'Blessed are
the peacemakers'; we have 'peace through the blood of Christ'; '*He*
is our peace'; 'for His name shall be called Wonderful, Counsellor,
the Everlasting Father, the Prince of Peace'. Think of the number
of times the word 'peace' comes in the liturgy and in the offices.
The second collect for morning prayer is the prayer for peace: 'O
God who art the author of peace'. The second collect at evening
prayer asks for 'the peace which the world cannot give'. Simeon,
when his eyes have seen salvation asks to 'depart in peace'. The
office of compline prays that 'asleep we may rest in peace'. In the
Eucharist we are offered the greeting: 'Peace be with you'; and its
final words are 'Grant us thy peace'. The benediction offers us 'the
peace of God which passeth all understanding'.

I have given all these examples because I want you to hear that word 'peace' struck like a constant bell - again and again and again in prayer and in benediction. I also want you to notice certain things about it, especially where peace *comes*. Peace doesn't come anywhere: it belongs above all to our comings and goings, arrivals and departures. It is very important to know the answer to the question: do you *come* in peace? It is very important as we leave to *depart* in peace. It is important in the pains of our last hour to make our peace. We pray for 'peace at the last'. Come in peace, go in peace; leave finally at peace, rest in peace. Coming and going, beginning and ending, nothing could be more inclusive and conclusive. Peace should frame everything.

But notice another characteristic of peace. It comes with other things. It is rarely asked for on its own; or thought to arrive except in good company. Consider the things with which peace comes: the words we associate with it, if you like. Peace, be *still*; peace and *quietness*. Peace has the association of stillness: it comes when men are still and know that God is God. 'Grace be unto you and peace.' Peace dwells with grace. 'Peace on earth and mercy mild'; 'no peace without mercy'; 'love, joy, peace, long-suffering, gentleness, goodness, faith, meekness, temperance': these are all placed *together* by St. Paul as the fruits of the spirit. So as we seek peace it is not to be found on its own but with the full fruits of the spirit. This inclusive thing, which frames arrivals and departures, beginnings and endings, can only abide in the company of the other spiritual gifts.

It is all these which, conjoined together, make peace *perfect* and joy *full*. William Blake, when he wished to portray the divine image placed peace *alongside* mercy, pity and love:

To Mercy, Pity, Peace and Love
All pray in their distress.

As Christ looked over Jerusalem, He said, 'If only thou hadst known the things which *belong* to thy peace.' Together with peace, alongside it, belonging to it, are a cluster in which are stillness, mercy, grace, and love.

If you are to have the peace of God, passing all understanding, you will have it, so says the benediction - *with* the knowledge and love of God. So, not only is peace at beginning and end, and not only is it in this ripe cluster along with all other fruits of the spirit, but it is grafted directly in the knowledge of *God*. It is fundamental; otherwise it is nothing more than a lull or a temporary escape. The lull comes sometimes; we manage the escape occasionally; but 'That piecemeal peace is poor peace'. A momentary peace is uncertain, easily fragmented and broken. Gerard Manley Hopkins compares peace to a shy dove, with shut wings, which roams around us but will not be caught and refuses to settle. We move to catch the sacred holy bird and immediately it slips out of our hands. If the dove is to descend and light on our heads, he must come with all his other gifts as part of the whole knowledge of God. He will not come 'piecemeal'.

When peace comes it comes to *dwell* and *rule*. One of the most miraculous words in our language, especially our language about God, is *dwelling*. 'Dwelling' means a completely settled and all inclusive presence whereby peace is housed in our hearts and minds. We are to become the place wherein the holy spirit has its *dwelling*. This is the same picture as we have of the incarnation itself: the holy spirit hovers, and finally lights, fills, and fulfils all things with a presence.

But we have to *let* it. We think we want it; but in actual fact we will not let peace happen to us. We talk about having a bit of peace but we dare not let ourselves be taken over by a *whole* peace. A *bit* would be quite enough. We imagine ourselves clutching at this elusive bird which refuses to settle; but really the dove cannot settle because we do not *let* it. Why? Because if peace settled and *ruled* our hearts we would be under an obedience.

Peace is a *rule*, which is why St. Paul tells us to let peace 'rule in our hearts'. Those who have truly sought and accepted peace have always obeyed a rule. We cannot have our will with peace; peace can only have its will with us. The bird of peace is kingly; the dove imperious. Peace rules.

Teach us to care and not to care
Teach us to sit still
Even among these rocks
Our peace in His will.

No wonder then we do not really want it. God's will is peace; He wills peace; but peace is when His will is done and the Kingdom come. We cannot have the quiet consummation without *finding too much*, altogether *more* than we can desire or ask. We do not ask it and dare not desire it because it will be 'a condition costing not less than everything'. We will not have peace at any price.

Which is why in the Christian religion the cost is God's. Since we cannot and dare not will peace, then peace will only come with a most bloody warfare of the spirit waged by God Himself. We have to see the cost in blood of our inability to seek peace and ensue it: for the chastisement of our peace was and is upon *Him*.

O Lamb of God that takest away the sin of the world
Receive our prayer.
O Lamb of God that takest away the sin of the world
Grant us thy peace.

Ecstasy.
Inside Heaven

'There is a little heaven of the soul, where dwells the
Creator of heaven and earth.'
St. Teresa (from 'The Interior Castle')

I want to celebrate the feast of St. Teresa of Avila and I take my text from her book *The Interior Castle*: 'There is a little heaven of the soul, where dwells the Creator of heaven and earth'.

We all have to use pictures to *break the sight barrier* between us and God. My imagination, that is my faculty for creating images, casts up symbols which mirror divinity. In the forum of my mind there are these visualizations, visual aids, videos, to bring before my inward eye what in truth 'no man hath seen at any time'. So, in one sense, God is out there, *un*-imaginably beyond all I may ask or think, and yet also palpably present in my imagination, in the pictures I have of Him. In this interior castle that is 'me' there dwells the creator of the heaven and the earth.

But most of the time this faculty is dulled. The mirror does not catch the light, the images are just blanks and the video breaks down. We just 'can't see it'. A dark night comes over the soul and we succumb to a desperate sense that there is nothing else besides distorting mirrors of our own selves. The creative world within and the created world without go blank.

Look closer at these revelations that come fitfully within our own interior castle. There is, I believe, a sort of scale or ladder of images set up in our interior castle from the diabolic to the divine. Let me begin at the bottom of the scale with images of hell: the devilish opposite of the angels.

A lot of what goes on in my mind, and I daresay in yours, is diabolical. There is there a hell such as the desert fathers experienced when their imaginations were infested with devils and phantoms. Inside our private theatre the screen shows nothing but phantasmagoria: deep holes where nothing is, traps with no exits,

148

appalling blow-ups of self, distortions, illusions of omnipotence, delusions of impotency. In among this ghastly crew of phantoms there are false spirits. And there is battiness of every sort. We think we hear the voice of God in our interior castle and it is only some mocking echo of ourselves, or some creaking wispy product of a false imagination. We lose our capacity to 'test the spirits' and are plunged in darkness. Perhaps some of you are given dream tours night after night of this world of will-o-the-wisp. This is the underside of the real world, the sinister regions where things that are *not* seem to *be*. It is the real absence of God.

But now let us go up the scale. We also know as we return to our senses, that in and through the ordinary natural world about us there are shapes and forms more substantial and more satisfying. We fix an inward eye on them and feel *arrested* by their compelling form, their pattern of growth and flowering, their fascinating individuality. As our eye lights on them, or as our inward eye senses them, we are drawn out of ourselves. They have *seized* our imagination, rescued it from phantoms, and installed their own beauty, or power, or mastery, or quietness. They *absorb* us. We are taken into a world of significant form which is marked by a stamp of authority. Artists open our eyes to this *authority* because they translate and transfigure creation for us. We see the created world once, and then we see it again transformed by the authoritative power of miraculous imagination. Each object, or pattern of sound or words, impresses itself on us as if it had its own secret and individual signature. Like Gerard Manley Hopkins we see the sweet earth unfold, plotted and pieced, clouds chivvying down their airy thoroughfares, the wind wrestling with ropes, the bird rebuffed by the gale. All these live in our inward eye, informing our selves, lighting up the interior castle. 'There is a little heaven of the soul, where dwells the Creator of heaven and earth.' But there is a further step on the ladder.

We live not only in this natural world transfigured by imagination, but also as men and women who walk in time, tell stories and cooperate in the vast collective venture of history.

There is nature; and there is human history. The key to that historical world is birth, climax, and death: announcement, frustration, and final fruition. We can see that world negatively as one damnable thing after another - damnation really lies at every point in the scale - or else we can see it transformed by great pictures of what it most truly is. Entry, exit, and re-entry are either the meaningless cycle, turning with mechanical fatality, or else the great turning points and forward redoubts in the redemptive drama. Perhaps in the end we 'don't see anything much' in birth and death, frustration and fruition. But faith tells its own, different story, putting before us, as the real tally of history, pictures of miraculous birth, transfigured life and redemptive death. It offers us icons for the inner eye to pass through and 'grasp God, throned behind death with a sovereignty that heeds but hides, bodes but abides'.

Heeds, but *hides*. He heeds you, yet He hides from you. Now you see it; now you don't. Yet, the feasts of incarnation, transfiguration, redemption, and resurrection for ever summarize the vision. Video. I see. And beyond the phantasmagoria of self and nothingness is the image in the soul which is the *light of all our seeing:* the express image and likeness of God.

In St. Augustine's words: 'Too late came I to love thee, o thou Beauty so ancient and so new - *pulchritudo tam antiqua et tam nova* - And behold thou wert within me'. Or as St. Teresa also put it: 'There is a little *heaven* of the soul, where dwells the Creator of heaven and earth'.

150

The Amen.
Truth and Finality

'The grace of our Lord Jesus Christ be with your spirit. Amen.'
Philemon 1 : 25

Earlier I wrote of blessings and cursings, and now I want to develop what I said then by looking at benedictions and particularly at *Amens*. Almost all the letters in the New Testament end with Amen, and most of them have some form of benediction. 'Grace be with you. Amen' is one of the most frequent endings and the simplest. The benediction which concludes the second letter to Christians at Corinth is the most famous and familiar one:

The grace of the Lord Jesus Christ
And the love of God,
And the fellowship of the Holy Ghost be with you all. Amen

There you have the germ of Christian experience out of which doctrine could grow. So benedictions and Amens are important, not just ways of signing off or bringing the message to an end. Even the gospels end with an 'Amen', though they lack a benediction. The Book of Revelation ends with *two* Amens, one following the benediction, and one before it, which reads: '*Amen*. Even so come, Lord Jesus... *Amen*.' Indeed, I think the Book of Revelation is full of Amens. After all, it is the last work in the New Testament, so you would expect many 'Amens' and 'Alleluias'. It is full, that is to say, of ascriptions: 'And all the angels stood round about the throne . . . saying *Amen*: Blessing, and glory, and wisdom and thanksgiving, and honour and power and might, be unto our God for ever and ever. *Amen*', or: 'I am he that liveth and was dead; and behold I am alive for evermore. *Amen*', or: 'Blessing, and honour, and glory and power be unto him that sitteth upon the throne, and unto the Lamb for ever and ever. And the four beasts said *Amen*'. These are more than ascriptions: they are *affirmations*.

So, in the New Testament we have a build-up of Amens. In

the gospels the narrative comes to a conclusion with this solemn word. Then in the epistles, even a simple one like Philemon, there is a benediction and an Amen: 'The grace of our Lord Jesus Christ be with your spirit. Amen'. And, finally, in the Book of Revelation there is a whole chorus of Amens and Alleluias: 'Amen, even so, come, Lord Jesus'.

Of course, Amen is not just a New Testament word. If we want the background to our Christian and, indeed, our liturgical use of it, we turn to the Old Testament. There are two texts there which give us the clues. The first is clearly liturgical and has to do with the coronation of King Solomon: 1 Kings 1 : 36. We use it in our own coronation service, glancing back three thousand years as we do so. The priest, Zadok, and the prophet, Nathan, come together in the solemn consecration of a king:

> And let Zadok the priest and Nathan the prophet anoint [Solomon] King over Israel; and blow ye with the trumpet and say "God save King Solomon" . . . . And Benaiah, the son of Jehoiada, answered the King, and said, Amen.

So here we have prophet and priest together at the solemn acknowledgement of a king. The liturgy is simple: 'God save the King. Amen'. It is a *ratification*.

The second text is also liturgical and has to do with the law. Moses is solemnly charging the people as to what they shall do when they cross over Jordan. What they perform then will be an act of obedience to God's commandment, and this is to make them God's people. So we have a moment of great drama. First, they are to have the law set up and inscribed: written in stone. Attached to the law are solemn curses. Each commandment and each curse is to be ratified: 'Amen'. If they hearken diligently to the law then they will receive equally solemn blessings. Evil is cursed; 'well-doing is blessed'.

Imagine the scene. The people of God stand upon Mt Gerizim and half the tribes are to pronounce the curses and half the tribes are to pronounce the blessings:

> Cursed be he that removeth his neighbour's landmark.
> And all the people shall say, Amen.
> Cursed be he that maketh the blind to wander out of the way.

And all the people shall say, Amen.
Cursed be he that taketh reward to slay an innocent person.
And all the people shall say, Amen.

This is the roll-call of the law, and Amen is the *ratification*.

What these texts tell us is this. There is the law, which all men shall solemnly ratify: Amen. There is the anointing of the King, by prophet and priest, which all men shall solemnly ratify: Amen. Without this law and this authority there can be no society. It is for the people of God to ratify and confirm by their united pronouncement. We can put it this way. In the Old Testament what we say 'Amen' to are those things which we may do as a community and as God's people. And we could not do without the law. The Old Testament may be surpassed certainly, but not abrogated or abolished.

So what change do we have in the New Testament, which surpasses the law? Do we say 'Amen' to something else? Is the last word different in the revelation of Christ? Yes it is. In the old dispensation our Amen ratifies law and kingship (or rulership), the foundations of our whole community; in the new dispensation our Amen ratifies grace, a community of grace, and the king and lord who rules us by his grace. 'The law came by Moses, Amen'; but we may also say 'The grace of our Lord Jesus Christ. Amen'. The Christian Amen follows the grace, just as the Jewish Amen followed the law.

Yet I suspect we often do not bother to ask what *is* this grace any more than we think about pronouncing the word Amen. We say the grace and the Amen like formulae; and our ratification of grace is just like the ending of any letter. Every weekday we compose letters thinking more or less about what we say, but when we come to the best wishes and the ratification we write like sleepwalkers.

'Yours faithfully', we write, but it is the most faithless sentence in the letter. It is the same with 'Yours sincerely' and 'Yours ever'. Every Sunday, or every time we speak of God, we say a benediction which speaks of grace, but we don't notice those last words, let alone bother about them. The ratification is automatic: a rubber stamp on grace. Perhaps we do not even know what we really mean when we sign off with a grace and an Amen.

Grace is simple, and means gift. The law commands and grace gives. That means that all the terms in the social covenant or contract of the Old Testament change their meanings. In the Old Testament the priest and the prophet and the king are ratified as God-given institutions. And so they remain. But in the New Testament what is instituted is the rule of one who is prophet, priest and king in the kingdom of grace, in the realm of the gift, in the community of love's sacrifice.

So the law is there still, given by Moses; and earthly rulership is there still, a King Solomon or whatever form of government we can think of. These are still to be ratified. But the kingdom of grace goes beyond these rules and these powers. Grace rules: demanding love not commanding law.

That last word in the New Testament, the mysterious revelation of John, is a vision of the power of the Lamb and its ratification by an Amen. The Lamb means the total, and all-sufficient sacrifice of love. Before anything *was*, there was a slaughtered Lamb; and at the end there is still a slaughtered Lamb. When the Bible speaks of the Lamb slain before the foundation of the world and the Lamb in the midst of the throne, it means simply; the first and the last word is this: God's gift, God's grace, God's sacrifice - in sum, God's truth. This is the last word, with which we conclude anything and everything we have to say: Grace, peace, and truth be with you. Amen has another meaning besides the final word of ratification. It is simply 'truth'. That little sentence at the end of Philemon could be translated even more simply: 'grace and truth'. For the law came by Moses, but grace and truth came by Jesus Christ. It is ratified; and it is true. Amen and Amen.

Epilogue:
The Sum of Worship

'This is my body which is given for you.'
St. Luke 22 : 19

Not long ago my youngest son was watching some strange happenings in Harvard University Memorial Chapel. He had witnessed that kind of thing before but he suddenly stood back and saw how odd it was. 'If we didn't know it was holy communion,' he commented, 'it could look very bizarre.' It could. So I want to try and find out what I understand by the strange act of Holy Communion.

I remember myself having a similar sensation of strangeness at a similar age. It had to do with an outrageous activity - singing from the Methodist hymn book. I had just read Freud's 'Introductory Lectures in Psycho-Analysis'. Normally the rows of respectable citizens singing:

Jesu, lover of my soul,
Let me to thy bosom fly

did not strike me as anything out of the ordinary. What more normal: even my mother did it. But after reading Freud I suddenly saw these sensible citizens as obscurely participating in some wild and bacchanalian revel. *What* precisely, I thought, are Miss Dorothy Rush and Mr. Arthur Collins getting out of this wild erotic language. Soon after that I read Sir James Frazer's 'The Golden Bough'. That was another shock. Holy Communion, I realized, could be seen as the act of absorbing and imbibing the powers of the dying God. Life for me was getting 'curiouser and curiouser'.

At the Holy Communion, the Eucharist, the Mass - whatever you call it - people behave oddly. They kneel in a circle to receive a crumb or a wafer which (they are told) is the body of Christ, a prophet of Galilee nearly two millennia ago. While that happens they may recite or sing a poem about a Lamb, the Lamb of God,

155

who takes away the sin of the world. That is pretty mysterious. If a visitor with no idea of the Christian religion were present you would have to explain to him that (for the believer) Jesus *was* the Lamb of God, who was sacrificed, and He *is* the Lamb who is worthy to receive all honour and blessing. The Lamb, you might go on to say, is central to the Mediterranean cultures in which Christianity was born. It was seen as innocent, it was sacrificed, and it gave sustenance to the people.

So when you come to look at it, Christianity is strange and even wild. Perhaps we should try to understand it as anthropologists, that is, as people concerned with the meaning of human actions and rituals. When an anthropologist looks at the eating of crumbs and the sipping of wine he sees something not strange, but very familiar. He knows about slaying the innocent Lamb and about drinking the precious blood. Blood stands for life and when blood is shed and poured out it offers vitality. And humankind has often thought that by eating a body, perhaps the body of a lion or a lamb, perhaps even the body of a man, you come to participate in his life and his vitality. This is your life and your vitamin. Primitives constantly gather around the stricken animal. So too Christians gather around the wounded lion of Judah, the dying Lamb of God, and the broken son of man. He does not die but lives in them.

And, of course, the anthropologist will say men are using the elements of bread and wine, flesh and blood, to talk with. This is basic sign language, this is *elementary* speech, because it has to do with the most basic elemental things, with our food and our drink and our bodies. This sign language is based on the simplest of all codes: to eat and to drink. To speak about life you eat, you drink, you absorb; and you use and offer your body. It is body language, and we all know about that.

But this is no ordinary eating and drinking, no ordinary 'body language'. These signs of life - the bread and the wine, the body and the blood - are very precious. They stand not just for any life, but for life at its most full and whole and unsullied. We know that our life is far from being full and unsullied: and now we come to share in that which is whole bread, whole wheat, pure and uncorrupted. So we bless the bread as standing for the best life, and we approach it with a purification of our hearts and our hands. The priest (or minister) vests himself to symbolize purification; in my own tradition he washes his hands. He perhaps kneels before the altar with his hands only just touching the top of the table, saying with or for the people: 'We do not presume to come to this thy table, o merciful Lord, trusting in our own righteousness, but in thy manifold and great mercies'. All these acts of purification and of heartfelt contrition show that we know how distant we are. We understand and acknowledge our corruption. 'We . . . bewail our manifold sins and wickedness.' And we make these gestures which tell of our distance from the whole, the holy and the good, in order that we may truly be made at one with God. We are abased that we may be exalted; we stand as Isaiah before the seraphim. We recognize we are very far off that God may bring us very near. We ask (that is) for acceptance and inclusion.

And then having made our approach by the cleansing of our hearts and perhaps also of our hands, we come to the table. Confidently, we take our places as accepted members of one united family. To share a table is to seal a friendship, to be ministered to and to minister, and to meet a host. This meal is most wonderfully hosted, by one who gives *himself* to us with his love and with his grace. Take this, with my love, '*This* is my body'; and *you* are my body. We are incorporated: taken into a fraternity of friends. This is the widest and most inclusive of all multi-national corporations: a body of men and women taking pledges of bread and wine together, who come from 'all nations and tribes and tongues'.

So *now* you may say it is all quite normal and understandable. Here is no problem. This is just the universal version of the family meal, the Lord's supper. Yet we look again at what we do and it becomes once more very strange. Consider these most mysterious words: 'He made there by his one oblation of himself once offered, a full perfect and sufficient satisfaction for the sins of the whole world'. And watch these most mysterious acts: the breaking and the offering up. We are not just celebrating a fraternal meal. We are holding up the body of Christ in the sign language of sacrifice. We are symbolically *re-enacting* the sacrifice of Christ by using our code language of bread and wine, body and blood. We are representing and re-presenting the last supper and the Passion. Here the danger signals start flashing. Are we then participating in a thinly disguised version of blood sacrifice? Do we believe in an angry father placated by the sacrifice of his son which we then repeat in every Eucharist? I hope not. Nevertheless I want to recover and re-use our profoundly sacrificial language and to understand what is meant by our offering up of the Passion of the Lord. I want to be able to say with Wesley in his great commentary on the Eucharist: 'Victim Divine, thy grace we claim'.

Think now of what men and women most seek: to be at peace, with themselves, with the world, and with each other. But that peace is not to be had just for the asking. We cry 'Peace! Peace!' and there is no peace. Why? Because peace would cost you *everything*. You will not pay the price of peace. No way. No way. The price of our peace is a profound chastisement, and who can possibly bear the chastisement of our peace? Who can bear it, and who can bear it away? There will be a death before there is a peace. The way through points to a death and a terrible sacrifice. We dimly sense through what garden agony the way of peace must lead. Somebody is going to have to walk into the wilderness and die, driven out and done to death by the weight of corruption and evil.

We are broken beings with broken lives. Ours is a fractured world, with a terrible split across the centre, and a wound at its heart. And this fracture can only be healed *by* a fracture, by that which is whole and perfect probing and entering into the centre of the wound until it breaks. The gesture of healing and love and of acceptance and redemption must be made at the very heart of the wound. The broken can only be met by a loving gesture which presses deeper and deeper into the heart of our brokenness until it is itself *broken,* at one with the wound. It is in the brokenness of the perfect image of God that the perfect image of man is restored. In the marring is the making. In the moment of agony, isolation and annihilation humankind is made whole. In the castaway and the cast-out man comes back to his peace. The moment of breakage is instantaneously the recovery of the whole. That is why there is a sacrifice and a breakage, because 'without the shedding of blood is no redemption'.

> Behold and see if there be any sorrow like unto his sorrow
> .... Surely he has borne our griefs and carried our sorrows.
> He was wounded for our transgressions, he was bruised for our
> iniquities, and the *chastisement of our peace* was upon *him.*

The cost has been absorbed: 'This is my body which is given for you'.

But that is not quite the end. The moment we participate in the broken bread all the wholeness and wholesomeness passes into our own body. We are enriched by this diet, we are at one in this at-onement, as His image is remade and reworked in all our human faces. We are, by grace, at-one with ourselves with our fellows, and with Him. Christ is, as Wesley put it, 'the Federal Head of all mankind'. I could not use more inclusive and generic language than that. And at this point all the images and pictures of feeding and offering and of enrichment and inclusiveness begin to converge.

At the beginning of the story it is the passover meal which celebrated the movement of Israel from enslavement and death to liberty and life. At the end it is the meal at Emmaus where the presence of the risen Christ was known to His friends in the breaking of bread. The marriage feast at Cana, the feeding of the five thousand, and the last supper all come together. There is the best wine created by Christ; there is the bread for the world which is miraculously multiplied till all are full; there is the divine bread broken at the last supper to feed our souls and bodies. The eucharistic sacrifice not only re-enacts the Passion of Christ but summarizes and resumes the whole narrative of redemption from passover to resurrection. It is the sum and the summary of what we believe.

It is giving and offering; it is breaking and making whole; it is incorporation and federation; it is distribution and sharing; it is the divine living presence known in the repeated gesture of love; it is the exhibition and demonstration of vulnerability; it is the feasting of all men and women in God's present and future Kingdom; and it is the passage from corruption to wholeness and from death to life. We are by our Holy Communion 'very members incorporate in the mystical body of [God's] Son, which is the blessed company of all faithful people'; and we are 'heirs through hope of [an] everlasting kingdom'.